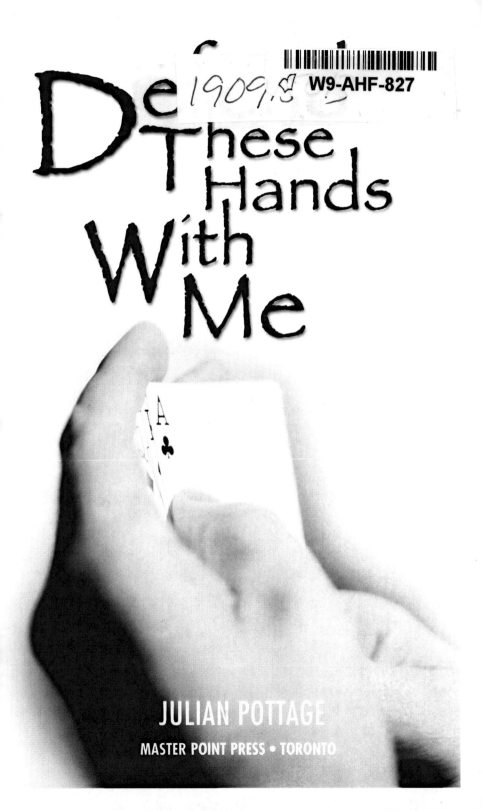

Defend
These
Hands
With
Me

1909.

W9-AHF-827

JULIAN POTTAGE

MASTER POINT PRESS • TORONTO

© 2006 Julian Pottage. All rights reserved. It is illegal to reproduce any portion of this material, except by special arrangement with the publisher. Reproduction of this material without authorization, by any duplication process whatsoever, is a violation of copyright.

Master Point Press
214 Merton St., Suite 205
Toronto, Ontario, Canada
M4S 1A6
(647) 956-4933
Email: info@masterpointpress.com

www.masterpointpress.com
www.ebooksbridge.com
www.bridgeblogging.com
www.teachbridge.com

Library and Archives Canada Cataloguing in Publication

Pottage, Julian
    Defend these hands with me / written by: Julian Pottage.

ISBN 1-897106-08-4
ISBN 978-1-897106-08-2

1. Contract bridge--Defensive play. I. Title.

GV1282.42.P68 2006   795.41'53   C2005-907219-9

Editor	Ray Lee
Cover and interior design	Olena S. Sullivan/New Mediatrix
Interior format	Luise Lee
Copyediting	Suzanne Hocking

2 3 4 5 6 7   19 18 17 16

Contents

Foreword

Over 5000 bridge books have been published but fewer than 200 of these contain collections of deals based on declarer or defensive play. It strikes me as odd that these books have not been more popular, as after all they offer the readers the chance to practice and so improve their technique. Although I think that many bridge players would like to develop their game, I suspect they don't know how to get the best out of the bridge literature in a way that suits them personally.

For my own part, I love any book that I can treat as a quiz because it gives me a chance to expand my repertoire of automatic plays. I like to try to solve each question, not in one reading but with several, over the course of a year or two. I find that when I see the problem a third or fourth time, I recognize it and so solve it almost at once.

This has great benefit when I actually sit down to play, because in many situations, whether as a defender or declarer, I have already 'seen' the problem at hand in a book. This reduces the effort I have to put in at the table and so reduces the number of mistakes I make. After all, a player is most likely to err when he comes across a situation he has not seen before.

This new book on defensive play from Julian Pottage contains a fantastic collection of deals to expand your repertoire. In particular, I am impressed with the way Julian introduces a fresh outlook on suit combinations, both in situations where there is nothing to indicate how to play the suit and, notably, where there has been a revelation in the bidding or the play. These are the problems I find a special delight for I am always surprised at the variety, novelty and application they have.

So, take advantage of your luck in having one of the two all-time masters of this format to test, and so improve, your game. Please join me in reading and re-rereading this wonderful set of new defensive problems from Julian Pottage.

Tim Bourke
Canberra
January 2006

Introduction

Most bridge players, unless they bid very aggressively, spend roughly twice as much time defending as they do declaring. Despite this, there are many more books written on declarer play than there are on defensive technique. I suspect that there are many more bridge lessons delivered on declarer play, too. Perhaps these are some of the reasons why many players handle the dummy rather better than they defend. I believe that the time has come to begin redressing the balance.

In preparing this book, another major factor hit me. Most players try to get by with the minimum of defensive signals. They might play high-low if they want a ruff or show a particular feature of their hands with their first discard. Often this is not enough. I had not chosen the examples for this reason, but you will find that on many of them my ability or my partner's ability to defeat a contract depended on more subtle signals. In other words, 'every card means something.'

Something else struck me in putting this collection together. Rarely does the solution depend upon a spectacular falsecard or other flashy play. Far more often you need to picture the unseen hands, working out what is and is not possible from the bidding and play to date. Then you need to identify which layouts enable you to defeat the contract and, if there are more than one, figure out which are the more likely. Then, if possible, you defend in a way to cater for several of these layouts.

The way I have structured the book means that you need not consider the deals as problems. Still, I encourage you to think about the next play whenever you reach a decision point. Many of these I have marked with a fresh diagram or a new paragraph. On some deals, an early play proves decisive but, on many, it merely acts as a preparatory move for the endgame. You need to stay on your toes either way. With rare exceptions I have not included any deals that are too difficult for anyone to expect to solve at the table.

I have arranged the deals so that you can focus on West for a group of fifteen deals, on East for the next fifteen and so on. Other than that, the deals come in no particular thematic or chronological order.

I would like to thank all those either directly or indirectly involved in enabling this book to be in your hands now. I must include all the partners with whom I defended the deals, some of whom have also helped in the checking, and my two proofreading stalwarts, Peter Burrows and Maureen Dennison. Others who have played a smaller part I may refer to at the relevant point in the text.

I would also like to mention the late Terence Reese. He not only devised the idea of the over-the-shoulder format but also it seems he did not suggest to any other authors that this particular book was one that needed to be written! Lastly but by no means least I must pay tribute to my long-suffering wife, Helen. The nine years we have so far been together have been the happiest nine years of my life. Without her support, I doubt that I would have been able to start this book, let alone complete it.

Julian Pottage
Porthcawl, Wales
January 2006

Instinctive View

When in fourth seat, do you ever try to guess what bidding will take place before it is your turn to bid and whether you would open if the first three players pass? I sometimes do, but I cannot remember whether this was the case when, as West, the following hand came along in a local Teams match with neither side vulnerable:

♠ A 6   ♡ 9 6   ◇ Q 10 7 5 2   ♣ K Q 10 7

North opens 1♣, which could in theory be a short suit. My partner, Graham, overcalls 3♡. Since we play weak jump overcalls, he should have a seven-card suit, but one can never be sure of these things. South bids 3♠ and I pass. North raises to 4♠ and two further passes follow. Again, I have nothing to say facing a hand that might offer no defensive values and 4♠ becomes the final contract. The bidding has been:

WEST	NORTH	EAST	SOUTH
	1♣	3♡	3♠
pass	4♠	all pass	

With the minors well protected and knowing that partner has the hearts, it seems natural to begin with the ace of trumps to cut down dummy's ruffing value. This is what you and I see:

```
                    ♠ K J 7
                    ♡ —
                    ◇ A K 3
                    ♣ 9 8 6 5 4 3 2
   ♠ A 6                  N
   ♡ 9 6            W           E
   ◇ Q 10 7 5 2           S
   ♣ K Q 10 7
```

It is usually gratifying when one has led a trump and dummy puts down a void suit somewhere. I need to restrain myself from smiling. Declarer plays low from dummy; Graham follows with the two and South with the four. I see no possible reason to change my initial view of the situation and continue with the six of spades.

DEFEND THESE HANDS WITH ME

Dummy's jack wins the second round of trumps when East and South produce the eight and five respectively. Declarer now comes to hand with the ace of clubs, collecting partner's jack along the way, and leads the two of hearts.

We play reverse count signals, making it an easy decision to play the six of hearts. Dummy ruffs, with the king perforce, and a club comes next. Graham discards the queen of hearts, presumably from A-Q-J (we are not going to defeat the contract if South has the two top hearts) and declarer, after considering the position for a while, discards a heart. My ♣10 wins, and this is what we can see left:

```
                    ♠ —
                    ♡ —
                    ◇ A K 3
                    ♣ 9 8 6 5 4
        ♠ —              ┌──────┐
        ♡ 9              │   N  │
        ◇ Q 10 7 5 2     │ W   E│
        ♣ K Q            │   S  │
                         └──────┘
```

Knowing that any time on lead as a defender may be critical, I pause to consider my options. With three suits to choose from, which do you think is best?

A club return I dismiss quite easily. Barring a strange distribution, declarer would be able to ruff that and then cross to dummy with a top diamond. A further club ruff would set the suit up, after which dummy's second top diamond would provide access to the established winners.

A heart return cannot work either. Declarer already has nine sure tricks — five trumps, a heart ruff and three top winners in the minors. The king of hearts would provide the tenth.

I shall have to lead a diamond and it scarcely matters which one if partner has the jack. In case South has this card, my diamond will need to be the queen. In theory, this also concedes a trick, but the suit will be blocked because South is surely 6-4-2-1.

Winning the queen of diamonds in dummy, declarer ruffs a club to hand and runs the trumps. I know to keep two diamonds and the winning club, and partner just needs to keep at least two hearts. This duly happens and, when declarer cashes the jack of diamonds and exits with a heart, East claims the last two tricks. This was the full deal:

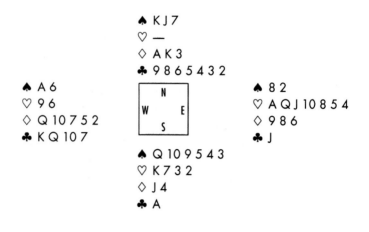

As it turns out, playing low on the first heart was vital. Had I played the nine, declarer would have been able to play three rounds of diamonds (ruffing the third) and then lead the seven of hearts to endplay East in a position like this:

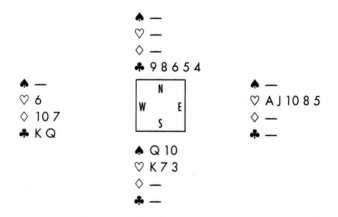

I would like to think that, even if we had been playing standard count signals, my instinctive view that the nine of hearts might be useful would have prevented me from going astray.

Remember the Serpent 2

Experienced declarers often try to give themselves an extra chance
by laying a trap for the defending side. You can often avoid falling
into such a trap if you have seen a similar position before. In third
seat, with only the other side vulnerable, this was my hand in a
knockout teams match:

♠ K 8   ♡ Q 8   ◇ J 10 9 8 4   ♣ J 10 7 6

Graham, my partner, deals and passes. The lady on my right opens
1NT, which they play as strong (15-17) at this vulnerability. I pass and
North bids 2♣, alerted as Stayman, asking for four-card majors. After
a pass from partner, South bids 2◇, denying one. I pass again and
North's jump to 3NT ends the bidding. This is the complete auction:

WEST	NORTH	EAST	SOUTH
		pass	1NT
pass	2♣	pass	2◇
pass	3NT	all pass	

With such good intermediates, the knowledge that South has no
four-card major (and hence is quite likely to hold four diamonds)
does not affect my choice of lead: the ◇J. Dummy comes down and
we can see this:

```
                    ♠ Q J 10 7
                    ♡ 10 7 2
                    ◇ K
                    ♣ K Q 8 5 3
      ♠ K 8              ┌───────┐
      ♡ Q 8              │   N   │
      ◇ J 10 9 8 4    W  │ W   E │  E
      ♣ J 10 7 6         │   S   │
                         └───────┘
```

Although she has no choice about how to play from dummy, declarer pauses to consider her strategy. I use this time to count the
points: I have 7 and North 11, and South 15-17. This leaves 5-7 for
East. The ◇A should be the most helpful card partner could hold,
and we seem to be off to a good start when Graham does indeed

capture the ◇K with the ace and return the six. Declarer covers this with the seven.

Clearly, I shall win the trick. The question is whether to try to convey that the suit is now solid apart from the queen (unless the six was East's last diamond) and whether to try to give a suit-preference signal. I also stop for a minute to consider that, since Graham has 1-3 points left, South must have the remaining aces, leaving Graham with either the king or jack of hearts but not both. Since he will probably not get in again, he does not need any signals but, to reassure him that the diamonds are running, I win with the nine and continue with the eight. After a second heart goes from dummy, Graham plays the two, confirming an original three-card holding (he would have returned fourth best from four). This time South takes her queen of diamonds. These cards remain in view:

```
                    ♠ Q J 10 7
                    ♡ 10
                    ◇ —
                    ♣ K Q 8 5 3
    ♠ K 8          ┌──────────┐
    ♡ Q 8          │     N    │
    ◇ 10 4         │ W      E │
    ♣ J 10 7 6     │     S    │
                   └──────────┘
```

Declarer leads the ♣9 next, but I do not feel too tempted to cover. It seems unlikely she intends to run this; presumably she is just unblocking in case Graham has a singleton ten or jack. If that were the layout, she would have a marked finesse on the third round and be able to run five club tricks — enough for the contract if she has the ♡K to go with her aces. As expected, she overtakes with the king and calls for a low club. Graham discards a low heart and, with a shrug, declarer wins with the ace. She goes back to dummy with the ♣Q and runs the ♠Q. The way declarer has played indicates that she needs only three spade tricks (or she would have kept a re-entry to a possible long spade). In this case she would surely repeat the finesse if I ducked smoothly, but now does not seem the moment to take chances. I win with the king, cash the ◇10 followed by the ◇4 and, disputing her claim for the rest, a club as well. This was the full deal:

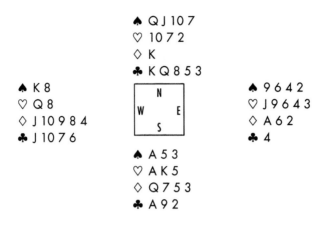

```
                    ♠ Q J 10 7
                    ♡ 10 7 2
                    ◇ K
                    ♣ K Q 8 5 3
  ♠ K 8                              ♠ 9 6 4 2
  ♡ Q 8              ┌─────┐         ♡ J 9 6 4 3
  ◇ J 10 9 8 4       │  N  │         ◇ A 6 2
  ♣ J 10 7 6       W │     │ E       ♣ 4
                     │  S  │
                    ♠ A 5 3
                    ♡ A K 5
                    ◇ Q 7 5 3
                    ♣ A 9 2
```

POST MORTEM

If I had mistakenly covered the first club, declarer would indeed have been able to run five club tricks, which would have given her the contract. As to whether I needed to play low smoothly. It pays to follow the Scouts' motto, 'Be prepared', if you can.

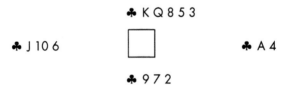

```
              ♣ K Q 8 5 3
  ♣ J 10 6       ┌───┐       ♣ A 4
                 └───┘
              ♣ 9 7 2
```

Now suppose the clubs were like this. It would still be right to duck the nine. Unless the bidding marks East with the ace, or declarer cannot afford to lose the lead to West (when nothing you do will deter her from taking the double finesse), declarer surely intends to put up dummy's king, which will lose to the ace. If you have wasted a high card on the first round, you will leave yourself exposed to a finesse on the second.

```
              ♣ A K 8 5 4 3
  ♣ Q 10 6       ┌───┐       ♣ —
                 └───┘
              ♣ J 9 7 2
```

The club suit has had more than just a tweak now, and this time South leads the jack rather than the nine. Again, in normal circumstances, the declarer intends to overtake in dummy rather than take two finesses, making it vital for West to duck. Moreover, on this layout, the ducking needs to be smooth: any hesitation would mark the position of the queen.

So Near and Yet So Far $\boxed{3}$

Knowing how to handle the dummy well is an extremely useful attribute to have as a defender. This certainly applies when it comes to squeezes. Unless you know what types of end positions produce a squeeze, you stand little hope as a defender of breaking them up. For a change, I offer you a hand on which we failed to defeat the contract, so you may wish to see if you can do better. Be warned, however, that this one is tough.

Second in hand and playing in a charity pairs, my hand is:

♠ Q 10 4 2   ♡ A 6 5 4   ◇ 10 9 7 4 3   ♣ —

The gentleman on my right, who is one of the best players at the club, deals and opens 1♣. With our side passing, North responds 1♡, South rebids 3NT and this is alerted. North raises to 6NT to end the auction:

WEST	NORTH	EAST	SOUTH
			1♣
pass	1♡	pass	3NT
pass	6NT	all pass	

North informs me that South should have a source of tricks in clubs to rebid 3NT. When I lead the ◇10, you and I see these cards:

♠ A K 8
♡ Q J 10 7 3
◇ J 5
♣ Q 10 5

♠ Q 10 4 2
♡ A 6 5 4
◇ 10 9 7 4 3
♣ —

```
        N
     W     E
        S
```

'Thank you very much,' declarer says, beaming. 'Play the jack, will you.' My partner, David, covers with the queen and declarer wins with the ace. He lays down the ♣A and looks worried when I start to think. Maybe his clubs are not solid after all. A diamond discard looks safe, but declarer will expect me to discard from my long suit, so I throw a heart instead. David follows with the nine, which, if it his second highest, means he started with J-9-8-x and does have a club stopper. Declarer leads the ♡K next and I let this win. He continues with the nine and overtakes in dummy with the queen. Do you think I should have taken the ace on the second round? It is too late to worry about that. I have to take it on the third, David discarding the ♠7. Our methods are to discard cards we do not want and to give count, if appropriate, as we do so. Needing to find another lead, these are the cards remaining in my hand and the dummy:

<pre>
                    ♠ A K 8
                    ♡ 10 7
                    ◇ 5
                    ♣ Q 10
  ♠ Q 10 4 2   ┌─────────┐
  ♡ —   │   N   │
  ◇ 9 7 4 3   │ W   E │
  ♣ —   │   S   │
                  └─────────┘
</pre>

Declarer's spade stopper for his jump to 3NT looks tenuous enough as it is, and he very likely has J-x; David's ♠7 certainly backs up this theory. Since a spade lead seems unlikely to break up a squeeze and will often give declarer a cheap trick, a diamond continuation looks right. I lead the ◇7, knowing that if both David and I have a third-round diamond stopper, we will be better placed to defend the end position than if one of us has the sole guard. I wait anxiously to see which card South plays on this trick and am delighted when the ace emerges rather than the eight. My pleasure is short lived, however, as the ♠J appears on the table. I should have been ready for this, and maybe a Chinese finesse by declarer is the only remaining hope for the contract. I elect to cover and the king wins.

I have no problem finding discards on the last two hearts, a spade and a diamond, but one cannot say the same for David. He discards a low spade and then parts with the ◇8. Soon my turn comes to feel the pinch. I discard a spade on the ♣Q and then wonder what to throw on the ♣K. 'I'll put you out of your misery,' South announces. 'If you throw the ◇9, my six is good. If not, then neither of you can have two spades left and dummy takes the last two tricks'. This was the full deal:

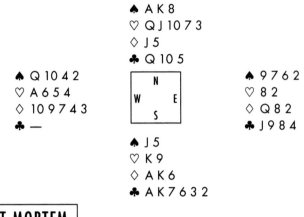

```
                        ♠ A K 8
                        ♡ Q J 10 7 3
                        ◇ J 5
                        ♣ Q 10 5
    ♠ Q 10 4 2          ┌─────────┐          ♠ 9 7 6 2
    ♡ A 6 5 4           │    N    │          ♡ 8 2
    ◇ 10 9 7 4 3        │ W     E │          ◇ Q 8 2
    ♣ —                 │    S    │          ♣ J 9 8 4
                        └─────────┘
                        ♠ J 5
                        ♡ K 9
                        ◇ A K 6
                        ♣ A K 7 6 3 2
```

POST MORTEM

This was the position after two rounds of diamonds, three rounds of hearts and one round of each black suit:

```
                        ♠ A 8
                        ♡ 10 7
                        ◇ —
                        ♣ Q 10
    ♠ 10 4 2            ┌─────────┐          ♠ 9 6
    ♡ —                 │    N    │          ♡ —
    ◇ 9 4 3             │ W     E │          ◇ 8
    ♣ —                 │    S    │          ♣ J 8 4
                        └─────────┘
                        ♠ 5
                        ♡ —
                        ◇ 6
                        ♣ A 7 6 3
```

East could see he would need to make two discards, and thus there was no point trying to hold on to his spade stopper. Unfortunately, if he had discarded both his spades, declarer could have made two spade tricks by finessing dummy's eight. Therefore, the contract was cold from here.

The only way to defeat the contract was to duck the ♠J smoothly. In that case, declarer, if he had foreseen the ending (a guard squeeze), might well have overtaken with dummy's king, playing East for spades headed by the Q-10 or Q-9 (or 10-9). On the actual layout, David could throw his spades away because my Q-10 would be a solid stopper.

Grand Clue $\boxed{4}$

In recent years, the standards for preemptive bids have fallen slightly. Many players take the view that the risk of losing a penalty, or of reaching the wrong contract if the deal belongs to their side, is a fair trade for making life as difficult as possible for their opponents. Fortunately, such matters did not cause any concern when I picked up the following hand:

$$\spadesuit \text{K 8 5} \quad \heartsuit \text{8 6} \quad \diamondsuit \text{8} \quad \clubsuit \text{K Q 9 6 5 4 3}$$

As dealer with both sides vulnerable, this seems a textbook 3♣ opening. North overcalls 3♡ and my partner, John, passes. South bids 3♠ and North raises to 4♠. South jumps to 5NT, inquiring about the quality of North's spades, and the 6◇ response shows one out of the ace, king and queen. South signs off in 6♠, thus ending the auction:

WEST	NORTH	EAST	SOUTH
3♣	3♡	pass	3♠
pass	4♠	pass	5NT
pass	6◇	pass	6♠
all pass			

To lead a singleton diamond when partner is most unlikely to possess an entry barely crosses my mind. I lead the ♣K and dummy is laid out:

```
                    ♠ Q J 6
                    ♡ A K J 9 3 2
                    ◇ 10
                    ♣ J 10 2
     ♠ K 8 5      ┌─────────┐
     ♡ 8 6        │    N    │
     ◇ 8          │ W     E │
     ♣ K Q 9 6 5 4 3 │   S   │
                  └─────────┘
```

Declarer plays low from dummy and John plays the eight. We play normal signals, making this consistent with a singleton eight or ♣8-7 doubleton. Declarer wins with the ace, cashes the ace of diamonds, on which John plays the six, and continues with the diamond seven.

```
            ♠ Q J 6
            ♡ A K J 9 3 2
            ◇ —
            ♣ J 10
♠ K 8 5        ┌─────────┐
♡ 8 6          │    N    │
◇ —            │ W     E │
♣ Q 9 6 5 4 3  │    S    │
               └─────────┘
```

Do you think declarer simply intends to take a diamond ruff in dummy or does an ulterior motive lie behind this play? My mind goes back to the bidding. South could have bid 4NT to ask for aces but elected to jump to 5NT instead. Surely this indicates a void somewhere, in hearts no doubt, and a hand with very few losers in all.

Rather than risk that declarer intends to ruff the diamond in dummy and discard the ♣7 on a top heart, I decide to ruff in with the ♠K and attempt to cash the ♣Q. If the ♣Q is ruffed, all hope of defeating the contract will probably come to an end, but there would be little hope anyway. Today my luck is in. John discards on the ♣Q and South has to follow suit.

The play ends swiftly after this. Declarer overruffs on the third round of clubs, draws two rounds of trumps ending in dummy and claims the rest. This was the complete layout:

```
                  ♠ Q J 6
                  ♡ A K J 9 3 2
                  ◇ 10
                  ♣ J 10 2
♠ K 8 5          ┌─────────┐        ♠ 2
♡ 8 6            │    N    │        ♡ Q 10 7 5 4
◇ 8             │ W     E │        ◇ J 9 6 5 4 2
♣ K Q 9 6 5 4 3  │    S    │        ♣ 8
                 └─────────┘
                  ♠ A 10 9 7 4 3
                  ♡ —
                  ◇ A K Q 7 3
                  ♣ A 7
```

As a rule, you should avoid ruffing with a natural trump winner, unless of course you think you can promote a trump trick for partner or you need to stop declarer from running a suit in dummy to take discards. I guess you also need to consider the possibility of ruffing to prevent an elopement or a trump endplay, but those situations occur infrequently.

In general, maintaining your trump length and strength more often proves an embarrassment for declarer. It is surprising how seemingly innocuous trump intermediates turn into winners once a few of the higher trumps have gone. To illustrate the rarity of needing to ruff with a high trump, consider the following deal:

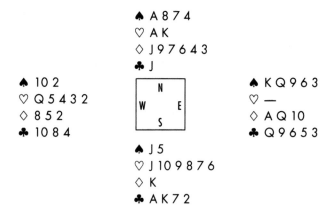

♠ A 8 7 4
♡ A K
◇ J 9 7 6 4 3
♣ J

♠ 10 2
♡ Q 5 4 3 2
◇ 8 5 2
♣ 10 8 4

♠ K Q 9 6 3
♡ —
◇ A Q 10
♣ Q 9 6 5 3

♠ J 5
♡ J 10 9 8 7 6
◇ K
♣ A K 7 2

After North has opened 1◇ and East has overcalled 1♠, South arrives in 4♡. West leads the ♠10 and dummy's ace wins. A low diamond goes to the ace and East continues with two rounds of spades, South ruffing.

On the precise layout given, or if West's hearts are Q-6-4-3-2, the sole way to beat the contract is to overruff the third round of spades to lead a trump. This stops the second club ruff and leaves declarer a trick short.

However, if we make West's hearts any better, discarding on the third spade proves just as effective. In essence, South can score one low trump by ruffing the second round of diamonds but thereafter has to ruff high. At the end, West will simply hold up the trump queen until South is endplayed. I leave you to work out the full details if they are of interest.

Alternative Method

One bright wintry morning, while scanning through my e-mails, I spot a correspondence between myself and my friend Martin in Florida. 'Can I give you a problem?' it starts. 'You are playing four-deal bridge (Chicago) in good company. You are West, fourth in hand, with only the other side vulnerable. You hold:

♠ A 10 9 3   ♡ 9   ◊ A K 9 5 3   ♣ K Q 9

'The first two players pass and South opens 1♡. You double, of course, and North responds 1NT. Partner passes and South rebids 2♠. You pass this time — I assume you can live with that — and North gives preference to 3♡. South presses on to 4♡ and everyone passes. I assume you agree it would be poor to double when almost certainly South has a singleton in one of the minors, which will kill one of your defensive tricks. Perhaps you would like the bidding in a diagram. Here it is:

WEST	NORTH	EAST	SOUTH
	pass	pass	1♡
dbl	1NT	pass	2♠
pass	3♡	pass	4♡
all pass			

You lead the ace of diamonds and this is what you see:

```
                  ♠ K 5
                  ♡ 6 5
                  ◊ 8 7 6 4 2
                  ♣ A 7 6 3
    ♠ A 10 9 3    ┌─────────┐
    ♡ 9           │    N    │
    ◊ A K 9 5 3   │ W     E │
    ♣ K Q 9       │    S    │
                  └─────────┘
```

'Partner plays the jack and South the queen. How do you continue?'
   I respond right away with a short query:
   'Are we playing standard signals or reverse?'
   'Standard,' Martin replies. 'Partner could hold either J-10 or the singleton jack.'

'Well, it may not make much difference. South, with presumably ten cards in the majors, is the one more likely to hold the singleton. We have a second sure trick (the ♠A) and possibilities for more. Assuming we have a club trick or a second diamond stands up, that gives us a third defensive trick. The setting trick will come if partner has a trump winner, J-x-x-x for instance, or if we can somehow stop declarer from ruffing a spade in dummy. If South has eleven cards in the majors, prospects look less bright. Partner probably needs the jack or queen of spades.'

'Yes, that seems a fair summary of the position. So what do you lead?'

'There seems little point in playing a trump because I shall not be able to play a second round. Is there a way to let partner discard a spade so that we can beat the contract even when South has solid hearts and the Q-J of spades? I could try a second top diamond but foresee problems ahead. Suppose it is ruffed and I come back in on the second round of spades, having just captured the queen of spades with my ace. This will be the position:'

```
                      ♠ —
                      ♡ 6 5
                      ◇ 8 7 6
                      ♣ A 7 6 3
      ♠ 10 9            ┌─────────┐
      ♡ 9               │    N    │
      ◇ 9 5 3           │ W     E │
      ♣ K Q 9           │    S    │
                        └─────────┘
```

Leading the ◇9 would not work now; that would set up dummy's suit. I have decided to play a low diamond at Trick 2.'

'Yes, that works if South is either 4-6-1-2 or 4-6-2-1,' he approves. 'In the former case, South has to ruff the second diamond and East discards a spade on the third round. In the latter case East ruffs the second diamond and again discards a spade on the third. You did better than the original West, who blithely continued with a top diamond. I shall give you the full deal now.'

```
              ♠ K 5
              ♥ 6 5
              ♦ 8 7 6 4 2
              ♣ A 7 6 3
♠ A 10 9 3      ┌─────────┐      ♠ 8 6 4
♥ 9             │    N    │      ♥ 10 8 4 2
♦ A K 9 5 3     │ W     E │      ♦ J 10
♣ K Q 9         │    S    │      ♣ J 8 5 2
                └─────────┘
              ♠ Q J 7 2
              ♥ A K Q J 7 3
              ♦ Q
              ♣ 10 4
```

POST MORTEM

For sure it was easier to find the way to beat the contract having been tipped off that this was a problem. Fortunately, the winning theme is one I have come across before. Consider this example:

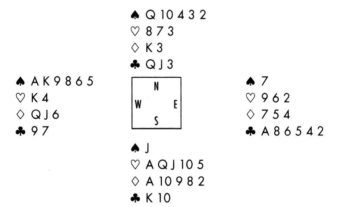

```
              ♠ Q 10 4 3 2
              ♥ 8 7 3
              ♦ K 3
              ♣ Q J 3
♠ A K 9 8 6 5   ┌─────────┐      ♠ 7
♥ K 4           │    N    │      ♥ 9 6 2
♦ Q J 6         │ W     E │      ♦ 7 5 4
♣ 9 7           │    S    │      ♣ A 8 6 5 4 2
                └─────────┘
              ♠ J
              ♥ A Q J 10 5
              ♦ A 10 9 8 2
              ♣ K 10
```

South, whose bidding has suggested 5-5 in the red suits, plays in 4♡. West, who has bid spades twice, leads the ♠A and sees everyone follow. Given South's likely shape of 1-5-5-2, continuing with the ♠9 surely offers the best chance to defeat the contract. A single discard is unlikely to benefit declarer because the club finesse, if there is one, is working. By contrast, enabling East to discard a diamond and so be in a position to overruff on the third round of that suit could make all difference. This way the defenders score the ♡K and ♡9 as well as their black aces.

Lead Not Wanted $\boxed{6}$

The play in a notrump contract usually follows one of two routes. The first and perhaps more common type is when one side or the other succeeds in setting up its long suit and this determines the contract's fate after a handful of tricks. The second is when neither side can get a long suit going, in which case the need to avoid giving away cheap tricks takes on a greater role and the play often remains meaningful until the bitter end.

Playing a pairs tournament in Brighton with my mother, Pam, I pick up the following collection in third seat with our side vulnerable:

♠ Q 9 6 5   ♡ Q 7   ◊ J 9 8 3   ♣ Q J 6

Partner passes and the middle-aged lady on my right opens 2NT. I pass and North bids 3♡, alerted as a transfer to spades. East doubles and, after two passes, a bid of 3NT from North completes the bidding:

WEST	NORTH	EAST	SOUTH
		pass	2NT
pass	3♡	dbl	pass
pass	3NT	all pass	

Obeying partner's double, I lead the ♡Q, and dummy comes down.

♠ 8 7 4 3 2
♡ A 9 6
◊ 10 7
♣ 10 4 2

<table>
<tr><td>
♠ Q 9 6 5
♡ Q 7
◊ J 9 8 3
♣ Q J 6
</td><td>
N
W   E
S
</td></tr>
</table>

When dummy plays low, East follows with the three and South with the four. It looks like declarer is concealing the two and that partner has played her lowest heart from five. Since the bidding makes her liking for hearts obvious, partner would have no reason to give an attitude signal. I play a second round of hearts and again dummy plays low. Partner wins with the jack and continues with the king, South playing the two and the ten. Partner's ♡J followed by the ♡K could be a suit-preference signal for spades. Still, if East had the ♠A, she would presumably play the ♡K and then the ♡J.

I have to find a discard and rule out a club straight away. A diamond also looks dangerous: if partner has the ♠K, South will need the three top diamonds to make up her total of 20-22 points. This leaves spades. It is often dangerous to weaken one's holding in dummy's long suit, but here the shortage of entries on the table makes a spade discard safe.

Declarer thinks for a while at this point and, when she goes into action, three rounds of clubs come quickly. Partner plays the five (showing an odd number) then the nine (in case her earlier signal for spades had gone unnoticed!) and finally the eight. We can see these cards remaining:

```
                    ♠ 8 7 4 3 2
                    ♡ —
                    ◊ 10 7
                    ♣ —
     ♠ Q 9 5       ┌─────────────┐
     ♡ —           │      N      │
                   │ W         E │
     ◊ J 9 8 3     │      S      │
     ♣ —           └─────────────┘
```

Now it looks almost certain that South began with a 2-3-4-4 shape. I also feel very confident that whatever strength partner has is in spades. This rules out leading a diamond because dummy's ◊10 would score. Do you think it will make a difference which spade I lead?

Clearly if partner has the ♠A, we can cash out for two down no matter what. This sounds unlikely, and the key spade holdings are a doubleton K-J or K-10. In the former case, it does not matter which card I lead now: even if partner plays the jack rather than the king, discarding the ♠Q on the thirteenth club will leave partner with the master spade. In the latter case, though, this will not work. The lead has to be the ♠Q. I do that, and partner plays the ten. Declarer wins and, judging correctly that my partner has the master spade, cashes out for one down. This was the full deal:

```
                    ♠ 8 7 4 3 2
                    ♡ A 9 6
                    ◇ 10 7
                    ♣ 10 4 2
  ♠ Q 9 6 5          ┌─────────┐           ♠ K 10
  ♡ Q 7              │    N    │           ♡ K J 8 5 3
  ◇ J 9 8 3          │ W     E │           ◇ 6 5 4
  ♣ Q J 6            │    S    │           ♣ 9 8 5
                    └─────────┘
                    ♠ A J
                    ♡ 10 4 2
                    ◇ A K Q 2
                    ♣ A K 7 3
```

POST MORTEM

'Can't you make that, sweetheart?' asks North, who appears to be South's husband. 'Knowing hearts are 5-2, you win the second round. You can play a spade to the jack and reach a position like this:

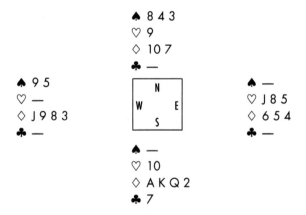

```
                    ♠ 8 4 3
                    ♡ 9
                    ◇ 10 7
                    ♣ —
  ♠ 9 5              ┌─────────┐           ♠ —
  ♡ —                │    N    │           ♡ J 8 5
  ◇ J 9 8 3          │ W     E │           ◇ 6 5 4
  ♣ —                │    S    │           ♣ —
                    └─────────┘
                    ♠ —
                    ♡ 10
                    ◇ A K Q 2
                    ♣ 7
```

West, who was able to get off play safely after winning the first spade by exiting to your ♠A, is on lead again having won the third round of clubs and has no escape. He does best to try the ◇J, but you win that in hand and cash the long club. To stop you from cashing three diamonds, he lets a spade go, but you cross to the ◇10 and lead a spade. West has only diamonds left and gives you the last two tricks.'

He is quite right, but try making it if East wins the first heart and finds a diamond switch. This is a tough play but by no means impossible.

Commitment Avoided

7

Against weaker opponents it may not matter if you defend certain types of ending inaccurately. They may lack either the ability to read the layout or the technical skill to take advantage of a helpful position. As it happens, however, the following deal occurred in the round of sixteen of the Gold Cup, Britain's premier knockout teams event. This meant that the opponents, who were probably either one of the original sixteen seeds or had beaten a seeded team, were no fools.

♠ A   ♡ A 7 2   ◇ K J 10 7 2   ♣ 6 5 3 2

Second in hand with both sides vulnerable, I open 1◇ after a pass on my right. North doubles and Graham, my partner, bids 1♠. South jumps to 3♡ and North's raise to 4♡ buys the contract. This makes the auction:

WEST	NORTH	EAST	SOUTH
			pass
1◇	dbl	1♠	3♡
pass	4♡	all pass	

A singleton in partner's suit seems an attractive lead and this is what I choose. Remarking that holding good trumps and only six losers justifies a raise, North puts down this 5-4-1-3 thirteen-count as dummy:

♠ J 10 8 6 5
♡ K Q J 6
◇ 6
♣ A Q 9

♠ A   N
♡ A 7 2   W   E
◇ K J 10 7 2   S
♣ 6 5 3 2

Graham follows with the two of spades. This presumably shows a six-card suit (we play reverse count, remember) because with only 15 points between the unseen hands, they should both have a bit of shape for their bidding.

    There is a singleton diamond in dummy and, if the spades are as I think, it is easy to picture a crossruff. If I thought partner might gain the lead, there would be a case for leading a low trump, to facilitate playing two rounds later. Since that does not apply here, I play ace and another.

A pleasant surprise comes: partner follows both times, with the four and five. Winning the second round in dummy, declarer ruffs a spade, which confirms my earlier reading of the spade position, and I discard the ◊2. Next comes a club to the queen, Graham playing the eight (middle from three presumably) and a second spade ruff. What do you think I should discard now?

```
              ♠ J 10 8
              ♡ K Q
              ◊ 6
              ♣ A 9
  ♠ —           ┌─────────┐
  ♡ 7           │    N    │
  ◊ K J 10 7    │ W     E │
  ♣ 6 5 3       │    S    │
                └─────────┘
```

Clearly South, who has jumped to 3♡ on a four-card suit, holds the ace and queen of diamonds, and I must aim to avoid having to make a losing lead in the endgame. Given that declarer is now out of trumps, keeping my fourth club as a possible exit card seems a good idea. This suggests discarding a second diamond. Regrettably, I see a snag because South is surely 1-4-5-3. Declarer will cash the ◊A, ruff a diamond, draw the last trump and come to hand with a club. Then, unless Graham has the ♣J, a diamond trick to me while dummy's blocking ♣A goes away will leave South's last club and diamond to take the last two tricks. Since declarer could draw my last trump in a minute anyway, I decide to underruff.

After the ♣J to the ace comes two rounds of trumps. I must keep three diamonds (at least) to stop declarer from setting up the suit, which rules out keeping both clubs. I would still prefer to keep one because that prevents an immediate throw-in. This means keeping three diamonds, and one will be the seven. It would appear we cannot beat the contract if South's diamonds include the A-Q-9 and, since saving the ◊7 will rule out ducking a diamond to me, my other discard is the ◊J.

Declarer, hoping my last four cards consist of the ◊K-10-9 and a club, cashes the ♣K and ducks a diamond. In practice, East wins with the nine and cashes the ♠K for one down. Here you can see the full deal:

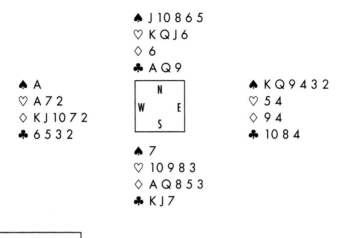

```
                    ♠ J 10 8 6 5
                    ♡ K Q J 6
                    ◇ 6
                    ♣ A Q 9
   ♠ A                              ♠ K Q 9 4 3 2
   ♡ A 7 2          N               ♡ 5 4
   ◇ K J 10 7 2   W   E             ◇ 9 4
   ♣ 6 5 3 2        S               ♣ 10 8 4
                    ♠ 7
                    ♡ 10 9 8 3
                    ◇ A Q 8 5 3
                    ♣ K J 7
```

POST MORTEM

As it happens, provided East held on to his ♣10, it would have proved equally effective to keep four diamonds at the end. The crucial move was underruffing the third round of spades in this position:

```
                    ♠ J 10 8
                    ♡ K Q
                    ◇ 6
                    ♣ A 9
   ♠ —                              ♠ K Q 9 3
   ♡ 7              N               ♡ —
   ◇ K J 10 7     W   E             ◇ 9 4
   ♣ 6 5 3          S               ♣ 10 4
                    ♠ —
                    ♡ 10
                    ◇ A Q 8 5 3
                    ♣ K J
```

Had I let go a club, declarer could have cashed two rounds of clubs and then two trumps to catch me in a genuine one-suit squeeze. If my last three cards were the ◇K-J-10, leading a diamond and ducking would then leave me endplayed. Keeping ◇K-10-7 or ◇K-J-7 would not work either: declarer would simply cover East's diamond with the same result.

Bite the Bullet

8

In any multiple teams competition, the standard of the field is mixed, even in the final. In order to win, you need a big score, perhaps 80 IMPs over 24 boards. Whether you achieve this may depend on having swingy deals against weaker teams. In one such event, in Eastbourne if I recall rightly, I picked up this hand as dealer with everyone vulnerable:

♠ K 10 4 3   ♡ A K 8 7 2   ◊ Q 6   ♣ 7 3

My partner Lawrence and I play a strong club system with control-showing responses, but we do not use canapé (bidding the second suit first) except when the main suit is clubs. Here, I open 1♡. North overcalls 2◊ and the bidding unfolds as below, with North's 3♡ asking for a heart stopper:

WEST	NORTH	EAST	SOUTH
1♡	2◊	pass	3♣
pass	3♡	pass	3♠
pass	4♣	pass	5♣
all pass			

At the five-level or higher, it is common to lead king from ace-king. This is because you will less often hold an ace-king and you might want to lead an unsupported ace. Accordingly, I lead the ♡K, and this is what we see:

```
              ♠ A 8 5
              ♡ Q 9
              ◊ A K 10 9 8
              ♣ 9 6 2
♠ K 10 4 3    ┌─────────┐
♡ A K 8 7 2   │    N    │
◊ Q 6         │ W     E │
♣ 7 3         │    S    │
              └─────────┘
```

My king collects the nine, the six and the jack. Unperturbed I continue with the ace, on which go the queen, five and three. In view of South's length in the black suits and reluctance to bid 3NT, it seems reasonable to place partner with an original holding of ♡10-6-5-4. His play in the suit, his second highest followed by his third highest, has been consistent with this. To avoid conceding a ruff and discard I need to switch.

Instinctively I work out that the setting trick must come from spades. South can have at most two diamonds, and dummy's ace-king will take care of those. In addition, any high club partner might have will surely either drop or fall victim to a finesse. Do you think I should play passively, or should I try to attack dummy's ♠A entry?

The strong diamond intermediates on the table provide the answer. If I let declarer draw trumps and cash two diamonds, a ruffing finesse will set up the suit. My opponent will hardly play me for ◇Q-J-x, both from restricted choice and because Lawrence and I play a weak notrump and five-card Stayman (meaning we would open 1NT with a 3-5-3-2 shape).

If, as seems quite likely, South is 4-2-1-6, there seems little hope even if partner has the ♠Q. In this case, the ♣9 will be an entry that I cannot dislodge. The best chance must come from finding South with a 4-2-2-5 shape. I switch to the ♠K.

Dummy's ace wins, of course, and declarer draws trumps. As I hoped, this takes three rounds, and I discard a heart on the third. After a brief pause, declarer cashes two more trumps. On these I discard my last two hearts whilst North throws two diamonds and East one card from each red suit. Next come the ♠Q and two top diamonds, but the jack does not fall. In a last desperate throw of the dice, declarer is about to finesse the ♣9, but partner shows out and I win the last trick with the ♠10. This was the full deal:

```
                  ♠ A 8 5
                  ♡ Q 9
                  ◇ A K 10 9 8
                  ♣ 9 6 2
 ♠ K 10 4 3          ┌─────────┐        ♠ 7 6
 ♡ A K 8 7 2        │    N    │        ♡ 10 6 5 4
 ◇ Q 6          │ W     E │        ◇ J 7 4 2
 ♣ 7 3              │    S    │        ♣ 10 8 5
                    └─────────┘
                  ♠ Q J 9 2
                  ♡ J 3
                  ◇ 5 3
                  ♣ A K Q J 4
```

After the ♠K switch, there was no way to make the contract. West's ♠10 was well guarded and East's third trump ruled out ruffing the fourth round of spades in dummy. Declarer might have worked out that I could not have only two spades, but finessing the ♠9 merely brought forward the inevitable.

Sacrificing a high card (here the ♠K) to knock out an opposing entry is known as a Merrimac Coup. In 1898, during the Spanish-American war, in an attempt to block the Spanish fleet within its harbor at Santiago, Cuba, the Americans scuttled their own coal carrying vessel, the USS Merrimac. The play derives its name from this.

One must take care not to confuse the Merrimac and Deschapelles Coups. In the latter, named after the whist and chess player, Alexandre Deschapelles, you lead a high card as a defender not to attack opposing entries but to create one for your partner. Here is an example of that:

```
                    ♠ 9 8 5 2
                    ♡ J 8 3 2
                    ◇ 6 5 2
                    ♣ J 9
  ♠ A K Q J      ┌─────────┐      ♠ 10 7 6 4
  ♡ A K 5        │    N    │      ♡ 7
  ◇ 10           │ W     E │      ◇ 9 8 7 4
  ♣ K 10 8 6 4   │    S    │      ♣ Q 7 5 3
                 └─────────┘
                    ♠ 3
                    ♡ Q 10 9 6 4
                    ◇ A K Q J 3
                    ♣ A 2
```

South, who has shown a red two-suiter, plays in five hearts doubled.

West, after cashing a top spade, has only one way to beat the contract by three tricks — to switch to the king of clubs. If declarer wins with the ace and plays a trump, West wins and switches to the ◇10. Nothing then can prevent East from gaining the lead with the ♣Q to give West a diamond ruff. Alternatively, declarer may duck the first club (playing one back has a similar effect), but West reverts to spades and perseveres with the suit each time after winning trump tricks. After ruffing three times, South is on lead and out of trumps. He loses a diamond ruff anyway.

Take the Money 9

In a serious game of rubber bridge, our side alone is vulnerable when I pick up this hand in fourth seat:

♠ 10 7 6   ♡ K J 9 7 3   ◇ A 8 3   ♣ A 5

After North deals and passes, my partner, a kindly gentleman with a wizened face, opens 1◇ in second seat. It looks like we might wrap up the rubber. The more rotund gentleman on my right seems to have other ideas and overcalls 2♣. After I bid 2♡, the next player passes, and partner raises to 3♡. Given our partial fit in diamonds I am ready to bid 4♡ and, when South bids 3♠, do so. Then, after two passes, South persists with 4♠. With such a flat hand facing a minimum opening, I do not intend to play at the five-level and double. This makes the auction:

WEST	NORTH	EAST	SOUTH
	pass	1◇	2♣
2♡	pass	3♡	3♠
4♡	pass	pass	4♠
dbl	all pass		

Since my club holding does not suggest an opposing crossruff, I lead the ace of partner's suit, diamonds. This is what you and I see:

```
              ♠ 8 4 3
              ♡ Q 6 5 2
              ◇ 10 9 2
              ♣ J 10 6
  ♠ 10 7 6    ┌─────────┐
  ♡ K J 9 7 3 │    N    │
  ◇ A 8 3     │ W     E │
  ♣ A 5       │    S    │
              └─────────┘
```

Partner follows with the king and declarer with the six. Partner could have played a less flamboyant card to encourage. Do you think he means the king as a suit-preference signal? In any event, my initial view not to worry about club ruffs in dummy appears correct. If we keep playing red suits, this will both force declarer to ruff and avoid taking finesses for him in the black suits.

Although continuing diamonds is a possibility, if I can make it safe for us to lead hearts from either side of the table, we may be able to make life very awkward for declarer. He has at most one heart and, given that his values probably lie in his long suits, this is unlikely to be the ace.

A switch to the king of hearts would spare partner from having to decide whether declarer has this card singleton. The downside is that dummy's queen will become good after two ruffs. Since I have bid hearts twice, the correct technical play of the jack feels right. If partner puts up the ace, we are no worse off than if he broaches the suit.

My luck is in and the two, four and ten of hearts go on my jack. Naturally, I continue with the nine, which collects two low hearts before declarer ruffs with the ♠5. After a little thought, he lays down the king of clubs. With these cards left visible, do you think I should take my ace?

```
                    ♠ 8 4 3
                    ♡ Q 6
                    ◇ 10 9
                    ♣ J 10 6
    ♠ 10 7 6       ┌─────────┐
    ♡ K 7 3        │    N    │
    ◇ 8 3          │ W     E │
    ♣ A 5          │    S    │
                   └─────────┘
```

Since there are three clubs in dummy, ducking to deny declarer an entry to hand serves little purpose. Perhaps, however, it could be right to duck if he has a finesse position in trumps. My thumb goes for the ♣5 when a thought occurs to me. If he really was keen to create an entry to dummy, why not lead low towards the J-10? This convinces me to take the ace; to duck would look very silly if partner has the queen. I play a third round of hearts and declarer ruffs with the ♠J. He plays a low club next and my partner does indeed produce the queen. Partner leads a diamond and declarer ruffs with the ♠Q. When declarer leads a third round of clubs I feel confident that partner has no more and discard my last diamond.

Sure enough, partner ruffs and plays a third diamond. Again declarer ruffs, this time with the king, and now he lays down the ♠A, to which all follow. He plays a fourth round of clubs and all is plain sailing from here. I have the ♠10-7 and the master ♡K whilst dummy has ♠8-4 and the ♡Q. If I ruff low, dummy can overruff but my hand is high.

A brief inspection of the pile of tricks on our side reveals that declarer has gone four down, giving us 700 when we take into account his 100 for honors. This was the full deal:

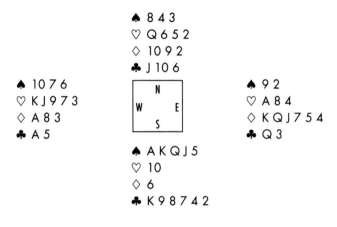

```
                    ♠ 8 4 3
                    ♡ Q 6 5 2
                    ◇ 10 9 2
                    ♣ J 10 6
     ♠ 10 7 6            N           ♠ 9 2
     ♡ K J 9 7 3                     ♡ A 8 4
     ◇ A 8 3        W       E        ◇ K Q J 7 5 4
     ♣ A 5              S            ♣ Q 3
                    ♠ A K Q J 5
                    ♡ 10
                    ◇ 6
                    ♣ K 9 8 7 4 2
```

POST MORTEM

Declarer took a calculated risk in laying down the king of clubs. He knew that unless someone held 10-9 doubleton in trumps (and he ruffed the first heart high), there was no way to reach dummy. It was a good plan.

For sure, North took a chance deciding to play in the 5-3 spade fit instead of the 6-3 (or possibly better fit) in clubs, but the gamble almost paid off. 5♣ would have gone two down, and 4♠ would have gone only one down on a trump lead. Indeed, if you trade the ♠8 and ♠9, a trump lead would actually allow 4♠ to make if declarer guessed the clubs right.

Some people say you should normally lead a trump against sacrifice contracts, but this deal and the postscript to the one before demonstrate the folly of slavishly doing so. If you have length and strength in declarer's side suit, or if you think the opponents do not have a source of tricks outside trumps, then by all means lead a trump. As a rule, though, a forcing game often proves just as effective against a two-suited hand.

After a break of several years, I find myself playing again in the EBU's inter-club knockout competition, known as the NICKO. The advantage of this event is social: you get to meet people you might not normally see. The disadvantage of playing unfamiliar opponents is that you do not know how good they are and what eccentricities they may have. In one of these matches I am in third seat with all vulnerable and hold:

♠ 7   ♡ 9 7 6 4   ◊ 8 6 5 3   ♣ A K 9 6

My partner, Sheena, opens 1♡, which promises a five-card suit. The lady on my right overcalls 3♠ and, whilst her red 'stop' card lies on the table, I consider my options. My normal rule is to allow myself to go one level higher than without the preempt. After convincing myself I would happily have bid 3♡, I bid 4♡. North bids 4♠ and two passes follow. Having stretched slightly already and not seeing this as a forcing pass situation, I pass to end the auction:

WEST	NORTH	EAST	SOUTH
		1♡	3♠
4♡	4♠	all pass	

I lay down the ♣A and dummy is stronger than we might expect:

♠ K Q
♡ Q 10 8 3
◊ A Q 9
♣ Q J 7 5

♠ 7
♡ 9 7 6 4
◊ 8 6 5 3
♣ A K 9 6

```
        N
    W       E
        S
```

Partner plays the ♣2 (count in view of the strong clubs in dummy) and declarer follows with the three.

Firstly, do you have a view on whether Sheena has a singleton club or three? The knowledge that South has presumably seven spades to East's three almost cancels out the fact that East has five more hearts than South. Perhaps South is more likely to be 7-0-2-4 than 7-0-4-2: Sheena needs the ◊K or the ♠A for her opening bid, and both unseen hands are more likely to have high cards in long suits than short ones.

It then strikes me that, if declarer is 7-0-4-2, we stand very little chance of defeating the contract. Suppose I switch to a diamond, that partner has the best possible diamonds for our side, a doubleton K-J, and that declarer elects to play the queen from dummy. Partner can win with the king but it will not be safe for her to knock out dummy's ace. After drawing trumps, declarer will play a second club and I will have to take my king. Dummy's two club winners will take care of her remaining diamond losers.

Just about the only way a diamond switch could work is if declarer holds an 8-0-3-2 shape with ◊7-4-2 and carelessly finesses the queen on the first round. Continuing clubs therefore has to be the right decision.

Assuming the opponents hold four clubs each, there can be no discards coming and it would appear safe to cash the king before delivering the ruff. All the same, I am conscious that if we take the first three tricks then the position will be right for a squeeze on my partner. Moreover, in view of her opening bid and my failure to double 4♠, declarer should not find it hard to place her with whatever other high cards our side possesses.

At first, it seems a squeeze will not work because both threats, the ♡Q and the ◊Q, lie in dummy. Partner, discarding after dummy, can cover both of those. Then I take a closer look at my diamonds: if declarer can find a way to have the diamond threat in her hand, say if she has J-x or 10-x, partner might be in trouble after all. Although declarer cannot afford to cash the ◊A to set up a simple squeeze, her ability to win the fourth round of clubs in dummy makes a trump squeeze a real danger.

I cannot say for sure whether my present opponent is good enough to spot and execute this but why take the chance? Having decided we cannot beat the contract unless Sheena has a singleton club, I lead the ♣6, which partner duly ruffs. She returns a trump and declarer draws trumps in three rounds before playing a club.

I take my king at once in case there is a discard available on the third round of diamonds and switch to the ◊8. A finesse of the queen loses to the king and the contract goes one down. This was the full deal:

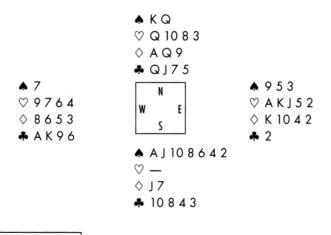

Had I mistakenly cashed the ♣K before giving partner her ruff, declarer could have run all but one of her trumps to reach a position like this:

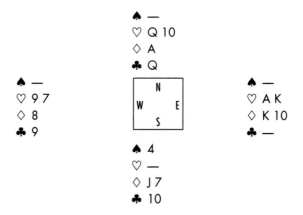

When declarer crosses to the ♣Q, what can East discard? If she throws a heart, declarer ruffs a heart to leave dummy high. If she bares the ◇K, declarer cashes dummy's ◇A and her hand is high. Admittedly declarer needs to work out what East has kept, but she has a complete count on the black suits and the bidding makes it highly likely the hearts are 4-5; she really ought to get it right if she has come this far.

Dual Purpose

The Crockford's Cup is the premier teams competition in England. Most matches are knockout, with an eight-team all-play-all final. In a tight match in the round before the final, with nobody vulnerable, I pick up this:

♠ J 3   ♡ K 7 2   ◇ Q 10 8 6 5 4   ♣ A 10

South, the dealer on my right, opens 1♣. My six-card suit allows the option of either a simple 1◇ or a weak jump overcall of 2◇. Given that most of my values lie elsewhere, I decide on 1◇. North bids 1♠ and my partner, David, passes. South rebids 2♣, and, when I pass, North bids 2◇. This may be looking for a diamond stopper or some kind of general force. East doubles, which shows the ace or king, and means I can lead the suit safely. South bids 2NT and North's raise to 3NT ends the auction:

WEST	NORTH	EAST	SOUTH
			1♣
1◇	1♠	pass	2♣
pass	2◇	dbl	2NT
pass	3NT	all pass	

I would have led my fourth-highest diamond without the double; I see no possible reason to do otherwise now. This comes down in dummy:

♠ A K Q 6 5
♡ 9 8 4
◇ J 9 2
♣ K 3

♠ J 3
♡ K 7 2
◇ Q 10 8 6 5 4
♣ A 10

```
      N
  W       E
      S
```

Partner wins the first diamond with the ace and switches to the jack of hearts. Declarer covers with the queen and I capture this with the king.

Partner's failure to return a diamond surely means only one thing — that he started with a singleton ace. Although this does not completely rule out reverting to diamonds, doing so will have to be with the aim of attacking opposing entries rather than setting up the suit.

South has bid and rebid clubs and is therefore highly likely to hold a six-card suit because, with a 2-3-3-5 shape, most players would either open or rebid 1NT. So, if partner's clubs are all low, the sole hope is that declarer started with ♡A-Q doubleton. Even if this is not the case, it could be a good idea to dislodge the ♡A: this card may serve as an entry to the long clubs.

The standard practice is to return one's highest card from an original three-card holding (some people call this 'remainder count') and I lead the ♡7. Partner puts up the ten and the ace wins. Declarer now leads the ♣5; these are the cards visible at this point:

```
              ♠ A K Q 6 5
              ♡ 9
              ◊ J 9
              ♣ K 3
  ♠ J 3            ┌─────────┐
  ♡ 2              │    N    │
  ◊ Q 10 8 5 4     │ W     E │
  ♣ A 10           │    S    │
                   └─────────┘
```

As a defender with an ace in the suit declarer wants to establish, one usually has two choices — play it early and try to block the suit or hold it up. Knowing the latter can hardly help when South has the ◊K entry, I go in with the ♣A. Now I must dislodge the ◊K. Leading a low diamond will not work because dummy will win; only the queen will do the job.

Declarer, knowing that ducking would not help, wins with the king as East discards a low heart. Next come three top spades and, as expected, South shows out on the second round. It does not matter what I discard because dummy is left with two losing spades and two winners in the minors. After the ♣K comes a fourth round of spades and partner takes two tricks in the suit to seal the contract's downfall. This was the full deal:

```
              ♠ A K Q 6 5
              ♡ 9 8 4
              ◇ J 9 2
              ♣ K 3
♠ J 3                              ♠ 10 8 7 4 2
♡ K 7 2         ┌─────────┐        ♡ J 10 6 3
◇ Q 10 8 6 5 4  │   N     │        ◇ A
♣ A 10          │ W     E │        ♣ J 8 2
                │   S     │
                └─────────┘
              ♠ 9
              ♡ A Q 5
              ◇ K 7 3
              ♣ Q 9 7 6 5 4
```

POST MORTEM

East did well to return the jack of hearts rather than a low one after winning the first diamond. He did not know that I had a club stopper and, from his viewpoint, one of the best hopes of beating the contract lay in finding me with the ace-queen of hearts over the king. True, if I held ♡A-Q-x, declarer could block the suit by ducking twice. Still, if you give your opponents the chance to go wrong, they will sometimes take it. On the actual layout, a low heart return would not have been good enough. Declarer would let that run round to dummy and, even if I held ♡K-10-x or K-J-x, his heart entry would be safe from attack.

Note how this deal illustrates trust in a partnership. Suppose I had held a fourth heart instead of the ♠J. In that case, it would have been vital for David to duck the second round of hearts to flush out the then unguarded ace. David trusted that I would have returned my fourth-highest heart if that were my holding and accordingly put up his ♡10 to drive out the ♡A. In a similar vein, I trusted David not to have a second diamond. Had South held a spade more and a diamond fewer, then my lead of the ◇Q would have proved a dismal failure.

The existence of this sort of trust in a regular partnership may explain why cut-in rubber bridge and, in recent years, four-deal bridge (Chicago) have never attracted many top players. Although you might say that the carding David and I used on this deal was sufficiently standard that you might expect almost all good players to replicate it, this is not so. Both Omar Sharif and Freddie North have recently written horror stories about their partner's apparent obliviousness to 'standard' carding methods.

Immediate Discovery

12

The Grandmasters Pairs in England has scoring by Butler IMPs — the best and worst scores on each board are ignored and the rest averaged to produce a datum score, with each pair comparing its results with that. My partner, Graham, and I are lying well down the field because neither of us is in the best of health. As dealer, with only the opponents vulnerable, I pick up:

$$\spadesuit\, A\,9\,7 \quad \heartsuit\, 8\,7\,2 \quad \diamondsuit\, A \quad \clubsuit\, K\,Q\,10\,8\,7\,4$$

I open 1♣ and two passes follow before the gentleman on my right reopens with a double. I might have opened with fewer clubs and less playing strength than this, so I bid 2♣. LHO doubles, and RHO alerts. It is quite common these days to play all doubles at the one- and two-level as for takeout; if nothing else, it avoids any confusion. A delicate sequence to 3◊ proceeds as follows:

WEST	NORTH	EAST	SOUTH
1♣	pass	pass	dbl
2♣	dbl	pass	2◊
pass	2♡	pass	2♠
pass	3◊	all pass	

I naturally start with the ♣K. This is what we can see:

```
              ♠ K 2
              ♡ A J 6 5
              ◊ Q J 9 6
              ♣ 9 6 5
♠ A 9 7        ┌─────────┐
♡ 8 7 2        │    N    │
◊ A            │ W     E │
♣ K Q 10 8 7 4 │    S    │
               └─────────┘
```

To my pleasant surprise, Graham overtakes my ♣K with the ace and returns the suit, South following with the three and jack. After I win with the queen, what options do you regard as worth considering?

Graham is a player who believes in bidding the full value of his hand and he can hardly have more than 5 points for his pass over

1♣. The only jack he could have is in spades, and that does not seem much use with the doubleton in dummy. Even if, quite out of character, Graham has passed with 6 points including the ♠Q, leading a low spade can serve little purpose because declarer would surely guess right.

Without a great deal of hope, I continue with the ♣10, and Graham ruffs with the ◇8. Declarer overruffs with the king and leads a low trump. I win with the ace perforce and am on lead with these cards still on view:

```
                        ♠ K 2
                        ♡ A J 6 5
                        ◇ Q J 9
                        ♣ —
        ♠ A 9 7      ┌─────────┐
        ♡ 8 7 2      │    N    │
        ◇ —          │ W     E │
        ♣ 8 7 4      │    S    │
                     └─────────┘
```

Since partner cannot have the ♠Q, he cannot hold the ♡Q either. This means the setting trick must come from trumps. On general principles, I cash the ♠A before playing a fourth round of clubs. Declarer thinks for a while and then asks dummy to ruff high. He draws a second round of trumps and, when I show out, concedes one down. This was the full deal:

```
                        ♠ K 2
                        ♡ A J 6 5
                        ◇ Q J 9 6
                        ♣ 9 6 5
     ♠ A 9 7         ┌─────────┐      ♠ 10 5 4 3
     ♡ 8 7 2         │    N    │      ♡ 9 4 3
     ◇ A             │ W     E │      ◇ 10 8 4 2
     ♣ K Q 10 8 7 4  │    S    │      ♣ A 2
                     └─────────┘
                        ♠ Q J 8 6
                        ♡ K Q 10
                        ◇ K 7 5 3
                        ♣ J 3
```

Only rarely can a player promote a trump winner for himself by ruffing. Still, that was what happened on this deal.

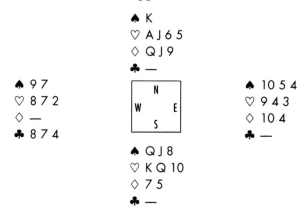

By ruffing with the ◇8 on the third round of clubs, East had cleared the king of trumps out of the way. This meant that, even though declarer carefully obliged me to expend the ◇A on low cards, the position was ripe for a simple trump promotion on the fourth club.

Here are a couple of other trump layouts on which partner might relish the chance to ruff:

           ◇ K J 10 5

◇ 7 2   ◇ Q 9 3

           ◇ A 8 6 4

If the bidding (or play) makes it likely that declarer will finesse East for the queen of trumps (diamonds), leading a side suit that East can ruff with the ◇9 will scotch that plan.

           ◇ K Q 10 9

◇ —   ◇ J 8 7 3

           ◇ A 7 6 4 2

Given the chance, declarer will cash dummy's ◇K to expose a marked finesse if either defender holds four trumps. You might thwart this if you can find a way to allow East to ruff with the ◇8.

Brave Heart

13

Playing in a good standard club pairs, I pick up:

♠ A K 3   ♡ Q 8 6   ◇ K J 9 2   ♣ A 10 3

I am in fourth position with both sides vulnerable. After two passes the bespectacled gentleman on my right opens 1♡. Q-x-x is not the world's greatest heart stopper but, with this shape and strength, any call except 1NT would be perverse. The player on my left doubles and my partner, Andrew, retreats to 2♠. We play that transfers are off after the opposing double; a transfer of 2♡ to show spades would give the opponents two chances to bid. It seems that they need only one anyway, for South bids 3♡, which North raises to 4♡. The bidding has been:

WEST	NORTH	EAST	SOUTH
	pass	pass	1♡
1NT	dbl	2♠	3♡
pass	4♡	all pass	

With awkward holdings in three suits, I am delighted to have an ace-king combination in the fourth and lead the ♠A. When dummy comes down one can see that North had a tricky first bid: a hand too good for a raise to 2♡ and too weak, given the likely bad trump break, for a jump to 3♡:

```
                    ♠ Q 8 5
                    ♡ A 7 5 2
                    ◇ 4 3
                    ♣ K 9 5 4
    ♠ A K 3        ┌─────────┐
    ♡ Q 8 6        │    N    │
    ◇ K J 9 2      │ W     E │
    ♣ A 10 3       │    S    │
                   └─────────┘
```

Andrew follows with the seven of spades (obviously count with the queen on view in dummy) and South with the jack.

Partner's even number of spades is clearly six and continuing the suit would establish dummy's queen for a discard. A diamond switch seems almost as risky for declarer could have the ace-queen. A club switch also looks dangerous. If South has the queen but not the jack, it would cost a trick. Although a lead from three trumps to the queen would often be wrong, here my 1NT overcall has given away the position and it looks like my safest bet.

Leading the ♡Q seems pointless, but do you think it might matter whether I choose the six or the eight? Well, the six may give declarer the option to win cheaply in dummy. It is not immediately obvious how this might help him: the only thing he could really do there is ruff a spade, and I am already unable to lead spades safely. Nonetheless, knowing it can hardly gain to give my opponent an extra option, the eight it is.

Declarer wins in hand with the jack, partner discarding a spade, and plays the ♡10. For the same reason that I led the eight, I duck this. Then the king draws the third round of trumps whilst East continues to discard spades. South now leads the ♣2 and these cards are in view:

```
                    ♠ Q 8
                    ♡ A
                    ◇ 4 3
                    ♣ K 9 5 4
    ♠ K 3          ┌──────────┐
    ♡ —            │     N    │
    ◇ K J 9 2      │ W      E │
    ♣ A 10 3       │     S    │
                   └──────────┘
```

Assuming South has the ◇A, partner will need either the ♣Q or the ♣J for us to defeat this contract. Since we have little to fear if he has the ♣Q, suppose his clubs are J-x-x. In this case, having won the first club with king, declarer will duck the next club to my ten and, after cashing the ace, I shall have to open up the diamonds. At that point, it would do no good to play a spade. Can you see why? Declarer, with a 1-6-3-3 shape, would have two discards, one on the long club and one on the ♠Q. It would not even matter who holds the ◇Q. If partner has ♣J-8-x, I can avoid the throw-in by playing the ten on the first round of clubs because this will create an entry for partner. Agreed, the ten will cost if partner has ♣J-x, but he would surely have discarded a diamond with a 6-0-5-2 shape.

Dummy's ♣K captures my ten, partner following with the six. A low club comes off dummy and East produces the hoped-for ♣8.

Declarer ducks this, hoping to flush out the ace, but it is not to be. The ♣8 holds and partner's diamond switch seals the contract's fate, the full deal being:

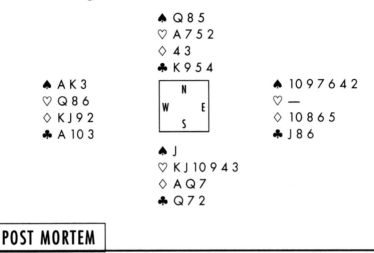

```
                      ♠ Q 8 5
                      ♡ A 7 5 2
                      ◇ 4 3
                      ♣ K 9 5 4
    ♠ A K 3          ┌─────────┐          ♠ 10 9 7 6 4 2
    ♡ Q 8 6          │    N    │          ♡ —
    ◇ K J 9 2      W │         │ E        ◇ 10 8 6 5
    ♣ A 10 3         │    S    │          ♣ J 8 6
                     └─────────┘
                      ♠ J
                      ♡ K J 10 9 4 3
                      ◇ A Q 7
                      ♣ Q 7 2
```

POST MORTEM

With all hands in view, can you see what would have happened if I had let the ♡7 be an early entry? Declarer ruffs one spade with a middle heart and draws trumps ending in dummy (still keeping a low heart). Then he plays loser-on-loser, leading dummy's ♠Q and discarding a club:

```
                      ♠ —
                      ♡ 5
                      ◇ 4 3
                      ♣ K 9 5 4
    ♠ —              ┌─────────┐          ♠ 10
    ♡ —              │    N    │          ♡ —
    ◇ K J 9 2      W │         │ E        ◇ 10 8 6
    ♣ A 10 3         │    S    │          ♣ J 8 6
                     └─────────┘
                      ♠ —
                      ♡ J 4
                      ◇ A Q 7
                      ♣ Q 7
```

If I lead a diamond, declarer's ◇Q scores. If I lead a low club, he wins with the ♣Q and plays one back to set up two discards. Lastly, with the ♡5 as an entry, ace and another club also gives him three club tricks.

Sauce for the Gander

14

'Here is a hand for you,' starts an e-mail from my friend Girish, who lives in Philadelphia. 'It's mainly a defensive problem but there's also a point on bidding theory. It comes from a recent Regional tournament and you are my partner. You are third in hand with nobody vulnerable:

♠ A 9 5   ♡ Q 8 6 5 3   ◇ A 7 6   ♣ 7 4

Your partner opens 1♣ and the lady on your right overcalls 1NT. You double and there is no further bidding:

WEST	NORTH	EAST	SOUTH
		1♣	1NT
dbl	all pass		

I write back: 'Girish, the bidding has ended and I've missed your bidding point.'

'Wait until you see dummy. You've probably guessed we are playing a strong notrump, which means the 1♣ opening could be on a three-card suit.'

'The ♡5 looks the right lead anyway. Someone who overcalls 1NT often has a strong holding in opener's suit, especially as she had the entire one-level available. So what makes the dummy so special?'

'Take a look.'

```
               ♠ 10 6 2
               ♡ 7 4
               ◇ 9 4 3
               ♣ Q 10 9 6 2
  ♠ A 9 5          N
  ♡ Q 8 6 5 3   W     E
  ◇ A 7 6          S
  ♣ 7 4
```

'Girish, I agree with you. 2♣ from North should be natural after this bidding. South has promised strength and implied length in clubs.

They might in theory have a ten-card club fit, which they should be able to play in. Anyway, what happens in hearts?'

'Partner wins the first trick with the king of hearts, cashes the ace and continues with the ten. South follows each time, playing the two, nine and jack.'

'I must win with the queen and I intend to cash the two long hearts. I guess I played the three on the second round to show my five-card suit. So, in case that might look like a suit-preference signal for diamonds, I shall cash the eight before the six to cancel that possible message.'

'On the hearts, dummy throws two diamonds and a spade, South a spade and a diamond and partner two clubs, the five then the eight. You are playing natural discards, with the first discard discouraging if it is very low or encouraging if it is a higher card. Later discards are probably count or suit preference, depending upon what partner thinks you want to know.'

```
                  ♠ 10 6
                  ♡ —
                  ◇ 9
                  ♣ Q 10 9 6 2
    ♠ A 9 5      ┌──────────┐
    ♡ —          │    N     │
    ◇ A 7 6      │ W      E │
    ♣ 7 4        │    S     │
                 └──────────┘
```

'East would surely find a way to signal more clearly if he holds the ♠K or the ◇K. Partner figures to have roughly equal holdings in spades and diamonds. I can't afford to lay down an ace to check and, if we do have three top winners now, they should not run away. I lead a club.'

'Declarer, who has A-K-x of clubs runs the suit. Partner discards the ♠4 then the ◇5, the ♠3 and lastly the ◇8. South discards the ◇J and the ♠J.'

'After discarding a spade and a diamond, I need to finish with A-x in the suit in which South has bared her king. East's high-low in spades, the four before the three, should show an even number in the suit, in this case four. So it is the ♠K that is unguarded and I discard a second diamond.'

'That's right. The contract goes two down, the full deal being as follows:'

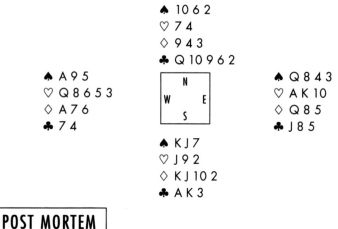

```
              ♠ 10 6 2
              ♡ 7 4
              ◇ 9 4 3
              ♣ Q 10 9 6 2
♠ A 9 5                          ♠ Q 8 4 3
♡ Q 8 6 5 3      N               ♡ A K 10
◇ A 7 6        W   E             ◇ Q 8 5
♣ 7 4            S               ♣ J 8 5
              ♠ K J 7
              ♡ J 9 2
              ◇ K J 10 2
              ♣ A K 3
```

POST MORTEM

It would have done South no good to unguard the ◇K instead of the
♠K: in that case West keeps two diamonds and one spade. These
were the cards left before the fifth club was played.

```
              ♠ 10 6
              ♡ —
              ◇ 9
              ♣ 9
♠ A 9                            ♠ Q 8
♡ —            N                 ♡ —
◇ A 7        W   E               ◇ Q 8
♣ —             S                ♣ —
              ♠ K J
              ♡ —
              ◇ K 10
              ♣ —
```

It would also have been no good for dummy to have kept two diamonds and one spade. In that case, East keeps a diamond more and
a spade fewer. There is a neat symmetry on this deal: East matches
dummy's length to maintain a threat whilst West keeps the opposite
shape to South to cash in on the squeeze. In a simple squeeze
(except the criss-cross variant), it is usually easier to know what the
victim has kept. It was the fact that North was going to lead the
squeeze card (making this a suicide squeeze) that prevented West
from cashing an ace to remove any ambiguity.

Narrow Door

15

The idea of playing opponents with the same score as you was used in chess before bridge. The concept has transferred well, with Swiss pairs and Swiss teams events popular amongst many players. In one such pairs match, my mother and I were playing a couple of New Yorkers on vacation in London. With only their side vulnerable, this was my hand:

♠ A K   ♡ A Q 2   ◇ 7   ♣ Q 10 7 6 5 4 2

South, the dealer, opens 1♡, five-card majors of course. We use weak jump overcalls, certainly at this vulnerability, and I must overcall 2♣. North raises to 2♡. Partner passes and South bids 2♠, a long-suit game try. Since the deal may still belong to our side in 4♣, I bid 3♣ now. A double from North casts doubt on that possibility and South's retreat to 3♡ ends the auction:

WEST	NORTH	EAST	SOUTH
			1♡
2♣	2♡	pass	2♠
3♣	dbl	pass	3♡
all pass			

I lead the ♠K (because of the A-K doubleton) and this is what we see:

```
              ♠ 7 6 3
              ♡ 5 4 3
              ◇ 9 5 4
              ♣ A K J 3
 ♠ A K        ┌─────────┐
 ♡ A Q 2      │    N    │
 ◇ 7          │ W     E │
 ♣ Q 10 7 6 5 4 2 │  S  │
              └─────────┘
```

Actually, I could have led the ♠K for another reason, as an 'alarm clock' lead, alerting partner to the fact that any switch might be to a singleton. If you play 'ace for attitude, king for count', you lose these options. In our actual methods, partner plays the two, presumably discouraging.

It looks right to continue with the ♠A for several reasons. Firstly, I may be stuck for leads on this deal and want to get rid of cards with which I might be thrown in. Secondly, it enables partner to give a suit-preference signal. Thirdly, there is a faint chance of securing a ruff.

On the ♠K, partner plays the ♠9, a high card suggesting diamond values and the inability to ruff a club switch. Since the bidding has already made it likely that if anyone has a club void it is South, I need no further encouragement to play my singleton diamond. For one thing, to lead the ♡2 at this stage could be storing up trouble for the future. For another, I do not want to lead a club if this will allow declarer to score two club tricks to which she has no entry.

Partner puts up the ◊K and this loses to the ace. Declarer now confirms my suspicions about the club position by leading the ♡K, which I win. These are the cards left:

```
                    ♠ 7
                    ♡ 5 4
                    ◊ 9 5
                    ♣ A K J 3
    ♠ —              ┌─────────┐
    ♡ Q 2            │    N    │
    ◊ —             │ W     E │
    ♣ Q 10 7 6 5 4 2 │    S    │
                    └─────────┘
```

If leading a club earlier was dangerous, doing so now entails even greater risk. Declarer probably has a six-card heart suit, meaning that partner has run out. If I led a club here and my opponent needs three discards (admittedly somewhat unlikely), a finesse of the jack would make this possible. Accordingly, I continue with the queen and another trump, on which partner discards two diamonds.

With no hearts lower than dummy's, poor South has to win the third round of hearts in hand. Three more rounds of trumps follow, but partner has no problems, discarding in total two diamonds, two spades and a club. After declarer cashes the queen-jack of spades and the ◊Q, partner wins the setting trick with the ◊J, the full deal being as follows:

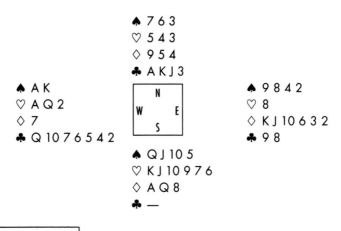

```
              ♠ 7 6 3
              ♡ 5 4 3
              ◇ 9 5 4
              ♣ A K J 3
  ♠ A K           N          ♠ 9 8 4 2
  ♡ A Q 2      W     E       ♡ 8
  ◇ 7             S          ◇ K J 10 6 3 2
  ♣ Q 10 7 6 5 4 2           ♣ 9 8
              ♠ Q J 10 5
              ♡ K J 10 9 7 6
              ◇ A Q 8
              ♣ —
```

POST MORTEM

In real life, we would probably have survived if I led the ♡2 after cashing two spades. Declarer would have needed to cash the ◇A before playing a heart back to take advantage.

The need to cash winners, and to cash them in the right order to avoid a throw-in, is a recurring theme when most of the defensive strength lies in one hand. Especially beware of retaining a singleton ace of trumps:

```
              ♠ Q 10 7 5
              ♡ K 10 5
              ◇ 9 6 2
              ♣ K 9 5
  ♠ A              N         ♠ 6 3
  ♡ Q J 8 7 3   W     E      ♡ 9 4 2
  ◇ A K J 8 5      S         ◇ 10 7 4
  ♣ J 7                      ♣ Q 6 4 3 2
              ♠ K J 9 8 4 2
              ♡ A 6
              ◇ Q 3
              ♣ A 10 8
```

South plays in four spades and West starts with a top diamond. Even if South is a moderate player, you can see why West needs to cash the ♠A before playing two more diamonds. If the third round of diamonds comes first, West will have no safe lead after scoring the ♠A. This will be so whether declarer has played three rounds of hearts or none, or two clubs or none.

Eric's Entry

16

If, in the mid-to-late 1970s, you had asked any knowledgeable player the question 'Who is the leading authority on the Acol system?', you could have predicted the answer: Eric Crowhurst. Eric is also well known for his contribution to the suit combinations section of *The Official Encyclopedia of Bridge*. He still plays the odd game, though not in serious competition. I would like to describe from Eric's point of view what happened on a hand that he held as East in a local league match.

♠ K 3 ♡ K J 10 7 6 2 ◇ A Q 7 ♣ 6 3

Only his side is vulnerable and the dealer on his right opens 1♣. This hand would suit an intermediate jump overcall just fine, but he must be playing either weak or strong because Eric overcalls 1♡. South then bids 1♠, showing a five-card suit (a negative double would show four). After a pass from West, North jumps to 4♠. Since North-South play splinters, this rebid suggests a balanced hand. It ends the auction:

WEST	NORTH	EAST	SOUTH
	1♣	1♡	1♠
pass	4♠	all pass	

West leads the ♡9 and this is what Eric as East can see:

♠ A 8 7 4
♡ A 8 5
◇ K 8
♣ A K J 10

```
          N
      W       E
          S
```

♠ K 3
♡ K J 10 7 6 2
◇ A Q 7
♣ 6 3

Given that the lead from 9-4-3 would probably be a MUD ♡4, it appears that West has either a doubleton or singleton heart. Declarer plays low from dummy and East naturally wins with the king.

There is some chance that partner can ruff a heart return, making this a suit-preference situation. Eric therefore returns the ♡J, the highest of his remaining hearts, to ask for the higher unplayed side suit, diamonds. Declarer's queen holds, however, and then comes another blow: a spade to the ace. This dashes East's hopes of winning the first trump with the king and playing a third heart for West to ruff or overruff.

With the club finesse, if there is one, working for declarer, Eric sees that defeating the contract would mean scoring one trick in each major and two diamonds. Unfortunately, four spade tricks, four club tricks and two heart tricks add up to ten, so defending passively stands little chance of success. For there to be only three club tricks to go with the six in the majors, South would need a 5-2-5-1 shape. Of course, in that case, declarer would surely have won the first trick and cashed the top clubs to discard the ♡Q. So, seizing his only chance, Eric drops the king of spades.

None too pleased by this development, declarer pauses for a while and then, with a shrug of the shoulders, plays a second round of trumps. West wins with the queen and leads a diamond. Declarer plays low from dummy, no doubt in the hope that West has the ◇Q, but Eric cashes his ace and queen of diamonds to defeat the contract by a trick.

Eric finds that his unblocking play earns his side a game swing. At the other table North played in 4♠ (unbeatable this way up) after a 19-20 2NT opening and transfer response. The full deal is as follows:

```
                    ♠ A 8 7 4
                    ♡ A 8 5
                    ◇ K 8
                    ♣ A K J 10
  ♠ Q 5            ┌─────────┐       ♠ K 3
  ♡ 9 3            │    N    │       ♡ K J 10 7 6 2
  ◇ 10 9 4 3 2     │ W     E │       ◇ A Q 7
  ♣ 8 5 4 2        │    S    │       ♣ 6 3
                   └─────────┘
                    ♠ J 10 9 6 2
                    ♡ Q 4
                    ◇ J 6 5
                    ♣ Q 9 7
```

Players become used to jettisoning high cards in side suits, say to avoid a throw-in, but many are apt to have a mental block in the trump suit.

♠ Q 8 7 4

♠ J 10 5   ♠ K 3

♠ A 9 6 2

It might be right to throw the trump king under the ace even with the queen in dummy. Suppose here that East is marked with the ♠K on the bidding and is keen for West to gain the lead. If so, East should drop the ♠K under the ace, which stops declarer from ducking to the king next.

♠ A K 5

♠ J 9 7   ♠ Q 3

♠ 10 8 6 4 2

In similar circumstances, East can drop the trump queen under one of the top cards to ensure that declarer cannot cross to hand and duck when West's nine appears on the second round.

A variation on unblocking is winning with an unnecessarily high card:

```
              ♠ J 8 7 4
              ♡ A 8
              ◊ A 8 4
              ♣ A K J 10
♠ K 5                        ♠ A Q
♡ 9 3 2         N            ♡ J 10 7 6 4 2
◊ K Q 10 7 2  W   E          ◊ 9 3
♣ 8 5 2         S            ♣ 6 4 3
              ♠ 10 9 6 3 2
              ♡ K Q
              ◊ J 6 5
              ♣ Q 9 7
```

West leads the ◇K against 4♠ and switches to a heart. Declarer wins with the king and leads a trump. To defeat the contract West must duck and East must win with the ace to return a diamond. Given that dummy contains plenty of entries for leading towards the ♠K, if declarer had the card, it does not appear too difficult to defend in the required manner.

Redundant Card

17

After we have finished a two-board round in a charity pairs event more quickly than most of the room, my partner, Gad, starts scribbling on the back of his scorecard. 'Can I give you a hand from last night's big game at TGR's?' (For the uninitiated, TGR's is the London club founded by Irving Rose, the initials standing for The Great Rose).

♠ A Q 5   ♡ Q 10 2   ◊ 9 8 6 2   ♣ K J 2

'It's the first deal of the rubber and you, East, are the dealer. You know I've told you that many of the people you meet playing for money bid cautiously. Well, the player who held your hand actually has a similar style to you and opens a weak 1NT. The hand on your left doubles and partner bids 2♣, natural of course at Chicago. After two passes, the doubler reopens with 2NT and the hand on your right raises. The bidding has been:

WEST	NORTH	EAST	SOUTH
		1NT	dbl
2♣	pass	pass	2NT
pass	3NT	all pass	

Partner leads the ♣10 and dummy goes down as follows:

```
            ♠ 9 7 6 2
            ♡ J 6 5
            ◊ K 10 3
            ♣ Q 6 4
        ┌─────────┐        ♠ A Q 5
        │    N    │        ♡ Q 10 2
        │  W   E  │        ◊ 9 8 6 2
        │    S    │        ♣ K J 2
        └─────────┘
```

Declarer plays low from dummy. What is your plan?'
      'Well, there may be a theoretical advantage in overtaking with the jack. Once partner gets in and plays the suit again, declarer will need to duck to block the suit. Mind you, this should not be hard because it may well be possible to tell from the bidding that partner

cannot hold the ♣K and a high card in another suit. It could prove awkward though if I can't play the jack quickly: one would hardly start thinking with K-J doubleton.'

'I'll let you overtake and declarer wins before running five rounds of diamonds. The ace comes first, then low to the king, next the ten overtaken by the queen. Partner, who started with the singleton seven, has to make four discards. These are the four of hearts, the nine of clubs, the three of hearts and the four of spades. Two low spades go from dummy. What are you going to do?'

'I might as well be honest. Play the eight on the first round, the nine as a suit-preference signal for spades on the second, the two on the third and the six on the fourth round.'

'You haven't said what you plan to discard on the fifth round.'

'Yes, that needs thinking about for a moment.

```
          ♠ 9 7 6
          ♡ J 6 5
          ◇ —
          ♣ Q 6
        ┌─────────┐      ♠ A Q 5
        │   N     │      ♡ Q 10 2
        │ W     E │      ◇ —
        │   S     │      ♣ K 2
        └─────────┘
```

Partner's high-low with the four and three of hearts seems such a gentle signal that it looks like it shows length, a four-card holding, rather than strength in the suit. With something like ♡K-7-4-3, it would be normal to discard the seven first. So, I put South with ♡A-K-x.

'Playing partner for the ♠K makes sense, partly because declarer spurned the chance to lead the suit when in dummy with the diamonds and partly because the ♣9 might have been a suit-preference signal for spades. After all, I knew the club position from the initial lead of the ten; a sequence in the suit scarcely seems news.

'Since on the last diamond I can't spare a heart and baring the ♣K may cause problems, I shall release a spade. It might as well be the ace.'

'Yes, that works. West with ♠K-10 left can now get in twice in spades when declarer exits in the suit, so can lead the ♣8 next and make a long club. This was the full deal:'

```
                    ♠ 9 7 6 2
                    ♡ J 6 5
                    ◇ K 10 3
                    ♣ Q 6 4
    ♠ K 10 4          ┌─────────┐        ♠ A Q 5
    ♡ 9 7 4 3         │    N    │        ♡ Q 10 2
    ◇ 7               │ W     E │        ◇ 9 8 6 2
    ♣ 10 9 8 7 3      │    S    │        ♣ K J 2
                      └─────────┘
                    ♠ J 8 3
                    ♡ A K 8
                    ◇ A Q J 5 4
                    ♣ A 5
```

POST MORTEM

```
                    ♠ 9 7 6
                    ♡ J 6 5
                    ◇ —
                    ♣ Q 6
    ♠ K 10            ┌─────────┐        ♠ A Q 5
    ♡ 9 7             │    N    │        ♡ Q 10 2
    ◇ 7               │ W     E │        ◇ —
    ♣ 8 7 3           │    S    │        ♣ K 2
                      └─────────┘
                    ♠ J 8 3
                    ♡ A K 8
                    ◇ 5
                    ♣ 5
```

In the ending as reached, a heart discard from East is clearly fatal, letting the jack score. A club, as I suspected, does not work either: declarer ducks a club and I can do no better than exit with a low spade; West tries a heart but South wins and throws me in with a spade to lead from the ♡Q. A low spade (or the queen) also fails: declarer ducks a spade and West wins to play the ♣8; declarer lets this win, however, and can then set up a long spade.

DEFEND THESE HANDS WITH ME

One Step at a Time

18

The Tollemache is an inter-county teams-of-eight competition played in England. There is intense rivalry between certain teams, typically those that border each other. At the same time there can be great camaraderie between the pairs within each team. The desire not to let your teammates down provides added reason to give of your best. During a match in which we had been trailing at the halfway point, you see me pick up:

♠ Q J 7   ♡ Q 10   ◇ A K 6 2   ♣ Q 9 7 4

I am the dealer with only the opponents vulnerable and open a weak 1NT. The gentleman on my left overcalls 2♠. My partner, Graham, passes and the lady on my right raises to 4♠. This completes a simple auction:

WEST	NORTH	EAST	SOUTH
		1NT	2♠
pass	4♠	all pass	

Partner leads the ◇10 and we see this:

```
            ♠ K 9 4 2
            ♡ A 7 5 2
            ◇ Q 7
            ♣ K 8 5
         ┌─────────┐
         │    N    │        ♠ Q J 7
         │ W     E │        ♡ Q 10
         │    S    │        ◇ A K 6 2
         └─────────┘        ♣ Q 9 7 4
```

Declarer plays low from dummy and my king wins. With most of the defensive strength in my hand, the danger of becoming stuck for leads later in the play is clear. Cashing the ◇A is the logical next move.

Declarer, who followed with the ◇4 on the first round, now drops the ◇J. Graham plays the ◇5, which looks like his original fourth-highest card in the suit and therefore is not a positive suit-preference signal.

A third round of diamonds would concede a ruff and discard, which I do not wish to do, and a trump lead appears incredibly dangerous. West figures to be void and this would create a finesse position for declarer. How do you read the other suits?

South really needs the ♣A for his vulnerable overcall and, in any case, if West has it, the contract will surely fail whether I lead a heart or a club. The ♡K also figures to be with South, and its position appears irrelevant anyway. If South has it, a heart lead should prove safe unless he has made an unsound overall with a 5-3-2-3 shape and holds ♡K-J-9. True, if West has the ♡K, a switch to the ♡Q might cost a trick if South holds ♡J-9-x, but that would be only a second undertrick.

Declarer wins the ♡Q in hand with the king, cashes the ♠A, on which West discards a heart, crosses to the ♡A and plays a third round of hearts. I am not ruffing a loser and discard a diamond whilst declarer ruffs. He continues with a spade to the king, on which West discards a diamond, before throwing me in with the third round of spades. After my partner discards another diamond, this is what we can see left:

```
            ♠ 9
            ♡ 7
            ◇ —
            ♣ K 8 5
        ┌─────────┐
        │    N    │      ♠ —
        │ W     E │      ♡ —
        │    S    │      ◇ 6
        └─────────┘      ♣ Q 9 7 4
```

Since South clearly has three clubs and two trumps left, I can dismiss the idea of playing a diamond. Which club do you think I should lead?

If South has ♣A-J-x or West has ♣J-10-x, then the choice makes no difference. The key situation arises when South has ♣A-10-x. In this case, if I lead low and declarer plays low, partner has to put up the jack, creating a finesse position against my queen. The 'clever' lead of the ♣Q crosses my mind, but if I play this, declarer will have seen 14 points in my hand and should know not to win in dummy and finesse. If he wins in hand and runs the trumps, that will squeeze partner in hearts and clubs.

By a process of elimination (if you will excuse the pun), I put the ♣9 on the table. Declarer does not seem too pleased with this card and pauses for a moment. Presumably, he is thinking whether to

put up the ace and run the trumps in the hope that West has
♣Q-J-x and will be squeezed in front of dummy. In the end, he
plays the ♣10, which partner covers with the jack to force dummy's
king. He then leads dummy's last heart and ruffs it high before
crossing to the ♠9. I discard my last diamond on this trick and show
my last two cards to declarer, saying that I will cover the eight or
duck the five for one down. This was the full deal:

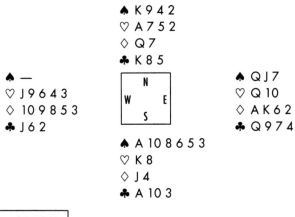

```
                    ♠ K 9 4 2
                    ♡ A 7 5 2
                    ◇ Q 7
                    ♣ K 8 5
    ♠ —                               ♠ Q J 7
    ♡ J 9 6 4 3                       ♡ Q 10
    ◇ 10 9 8 5 3                      ◇ A K 6 2
    ♣ J 6 2                           ♣ Q 9 7 4
                    ♠ A 10 8 6 5 3
                    ♡ K 8
                    ◇ J 4
                    ♣ A 10 3
```

POST MORTEM

You may have noticed on this deal that my correct exit in clubs, the
nine from Q-9-7-x, was the same card I would have led earlier in the
play if partner could have had an entry and we wanted to set up a
club trick. You may hear this referred to as a 'surrounding' play,
because the holding includes the cards just above and below
dummy's eight. Now imagine that the lie of the cards was a little
different:

```
                    ♣ K 8 5
    ♣ J 4 2                           ♣ Q 9 6 3
                    ♣ A 10 7
```

Imagine also that my sole concern is not giving declarer three club
tricks when I am forced to break this new layout of the club suit.
Leading the nine would work fine if West has J-7-x, but not so well
when South has A-10-7. Only the lead of the queen stops declarer
from taking three club tricks by force.

Privileged Information

19

Usually, when playing on a team of more than four and sitting out, I will try to rest rather than watching the others in action. Apart from the benefit of conserving my energy, it can be very frustrating to watch a teammate make what one thinks is a mistake and be helpless to do anything about it. I might make an exception in the last set. Such was the case on the hand you are about to see when I decided to watch David. He picked up the following hand, vulnerable against not, in fourth seat:

♠ —   ♡ Q 10 7 4 3   ◇ K 9 7 2   ♣ Q 7 5 2

His opponents conducted a lengthy uncontested auction to 6♠ as follows:

WEST	NORTH	EAST	SOUTH
			1♠
pass	2NT	pass	3♠
pass	4◇	pass	4♡
pass	4NT	pass	5♡
pass	5NT	pass	6♡
pass	6♠	all pass	

2NT is a game forcing spade raise, 3♠ is waiting, 4◇ and 4♡ are cuebids, 5♡ shows two keycards without the ♠Q and 6♡ shows the ♡K. West leads the ♣3 and dummy comes down:

♠ A K Q 10 3
♡ J 9 2
◇ A Q 6
♣ K J

```
        N
    W       E
        S
```

♠ —
♡ Q 10 7 4 3
◇ K 9 7 2
♣ Q 7 5 2

Declarer calls for the jack and captures David's queen with the ace. Three rounds of trumps come next; West follows each time and I watch as David discards the ♡3, the ♡4 and the ♣5. Declarer continues with the king of clubs, a heart to the ace, the king of hearts and a club ruff.

```
        ♠ 10
        ♡ J
        ◇ A Q 6
        ♣ —
    ┌─────────┐      ♠ —
    │    N    │      ♡ Q
    │ W     E │      ◇ K 9 7 2
    │    S    │      ♣ —
    └─────────┘
```

Next comes the ♡J, covered and ruffed, and declarer leads a diamond. West plays the eight and East captures dummy's queen with his king. David returns the nine of diamonds and South, after a brief pause, covers with the ten. West produces the jack and the ace wins. A trump takes the next trick but David wins the last trick with the seven of diamonds to put the contract one down. This is the full deal:

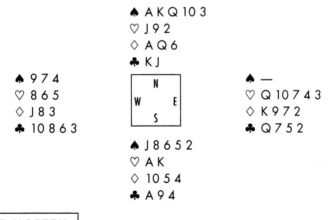

```
                    ♠ A K Q 10 3
                    ♡ J 9 2
                    ◇ A Q 6
                    ♣ K J
    ♠ 9 7 4      ┌─────────┐      ♠ —
    ♡ 8 6 5      │    N    │      ♡ Q 10 7 4 3
    ◇ J 8 3      │ W     E │      ◇ K 9 7 2
    ♣ 10 8 6 3   │    S    │      ♣ Q 7 5 2
                 └─────────┘
                    ♠ J 8 6 5 2
                    ♡ A K
                    ◇ 10 5 4
                    ♣ A 9 4
```

POST MORTEM

The defenders did well at the end, West by rising with the ◇8 to prevent declarer from ducking the trick to East, and East by returning the ◇9 rather than the two. South did the right thing in putting up the ◇10. Ducking would only work if West had the singleton ◇J left. If the diamonds were 2-5, then the odds would be five to two that East held the jack.

Rixi Markus famously remarked that many contracts that are made could be defeated and many defeated contracts could be made. You may have already worked out the validity of the second part of her statement in relation to this deal. Perhaps we can look at the five-card ending again:

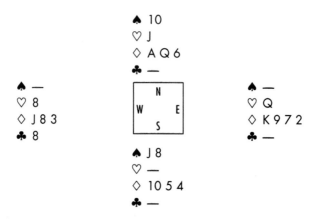

```
                  ♠ 10
                  ♡ J
                  ◇ A Q 6
                  ♣ —
  ♠ —                        ♠ —
  ♡ 8              ┌─────┐    ♡ Q
  ◇ J 8 3          │ N   │    ◇ K 9 7 2
  ♣ 8            W │     │ E  ♣ —
                   │   S │
                  └─────┘
                  ♠ J 8
                  ♡ —
                  ◇ 10 5 4
                  ♣ —
```

When East plays the ♡Q on the ♡J, declarer simply needs to discard a diamond! Whether East returns a diamond into the ace-queen or gives a ruff and discard (not that he can from this position), the slam makes.

Nevertheless, I contend that the slam ought to fail, giving credence to the first part of Rixi's remark. Since we have already noted that East did not need his ◇2 in the end position, why not keep a heart more and a diamond less? He can count declarer for eleven sure tricks: five spades, two hearts (South needs the ♡K to have an opening bid), one diamond, two clubs and a club ruff (the lead of the ♣3 having marked South with at least three clubs). East can therefore work out that there is no hope if South holds a 5-3-2-3 shape: if that is the case, East cannot avoid being endplayed with the third round of hearts.

In other words, East does not want to win the third round of hearts with the queen. He wants South to be in a position to ruff and actually to do so. East should therefore keep a low heart with the queen and play that low heart if declarer strips the clubs before the third round of hearts. Most people, on seeing East play low on the third round of hearts, will place West with the ♡Q. It will then be normal to look for a line to cater for this. Here, with ◇10-x-x, declarer has a realistic chance of a throw-in. For it to work, East simply needs the ◇J. I'm pretty sure I know what the vast majority of declarers would do if they were forced guess whether East has the ♡Q or the ◇J.

Clear the Way

20

Duplicate players, by and large, spend a lot of time playing match-point pairs. With this scoring method, it can be as big a bottom to collect 500 when the rest of the field has 620 as it would be to lose 100. This makes the relative size of a score important rather than its absolute value. In contrast, rubber players, or at any rate the successful ones, will not worry about collecting 500 when game might be on. They are happy to take the plus and tend to be good judges of when to double their opponents. Playing rubber bridge in decent company I pick up:

♠ J 5   ♡ A K J 8 3 2   ◇ 2   ♣ Q 7 5 3

I am third in hand with all vulnerable and partner, West, opens 1♠. After North passes, I bid 2♡ and South bids 3◇. When partner doubles, North passes and I do the same. Nobody expects me to have many diamonds if South has a vulnerable three-level overcall and West a penalty double; I do have a trump and am happy with a heart lead. The bidding has been:

WEST	NORTH	EAST	SOUTH
1♠	pass	2♡	3◇
dbl	all pass		

Partner leads the ♡9 and this is what you and I see:

```
            ♠ 7 6 4 3
            ♡ 10 7
            ◇ J
            ♣ K J 9 8 4 2
         ┌───────────┐
         │     N     │        ♠ J 5
         │ W       E │        ♡ A K J 8 3 2
         │     S     │        ◇ 2
         └───────────┘        ♣ Q 7 5 3
```

My play to the first trick is easy: win with the king. I can see that I shall not have the lead many more times and pause to consider my options.

A heart continuation seems unattractive: I would set up South's queen and the ◊J stands ready in dummy to ruff the third round of the suit. A trump merits brief consideration; it cannot give a trick away and a lead through declarer may be helpful. Of course, since dummy has just one trump, a trump switch after getting back in on the second round of hearts should prove equally effective in preventing ruffs. The only immediately obvious purpose of leading a club is that it will stop partner from ducking (and hence losing) the ace if declarer has a singleton club.

A spade is my choice. The absence of an initial spade lead makes it likely partner has the ace-queen and a lead of the suit from me should allow partner several easy exits in the suit. The king and ace cover my ♠J and partner cashes the ♠Q. He plays a third round of spades and I discard the ♡8. My heart strength is already clear and declarer may well know how many hearts I hold, which means it makes sense to give an accurate count signal. Declarer ruffs the third spade and tries a club.

Once I have turned up with the ace-king of hearts, it is fairly clear that I am not going to have the ♣A as well. Accordingly, partner goes in with the ace. Since it might be right for our side to play a second round of clubs if South started with a doubleton, again I give a true count signal and follow with the ♣7.

Partner, a young man who may be a professional player, thinks for a while before leading to the next trick with the ◊K. Declarer wins with the ace and returns the ◊6. Partner wins with the eight and, after I discard a heart, reverts to spades. I discard a club this time.

Declarer ruffs this fourth round of spades before playing the queen and a low trump to partner's ten. Dummy and I are still to discard in this position:

```
              ♠ —
              ♡ 10
              ◊ —
              ♣ K J 9
         ┌─────────┐          ♠ —
         │    N    │          ♡ A J
         │ W     E │          ◊ —
         │    S    │          ♣ Q 5
         └─────────┘
```

DEFEND THESE HANDS WITH ME

If partner has another trump left, my play does not matter. If his other non-spade is a heart, we get all the rest; if not, the ♣K must score. If he is out of trumps though, I must keep both hearts. If I do not, declarer could ruff the next spade and play a heart, forcing me to concede the last trick to the ♣K. So, I discard a club. Partner plays his last spade next and declarer throws a heart (no doubt in the hope West is out of hearts). In practice, my ♡A wins the penultimate trick and we have 1100. This was the full deal:

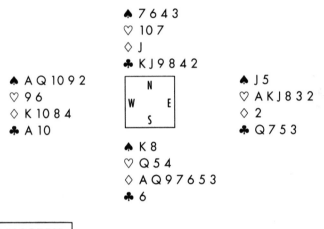

```
                    ♠ 7 6 4 3
                    ♡ 10 7
                    ◊ J
                    ♣ K J 9 8 4 2
  ♠ A Q 10 9 2         ┌─────────┐        ♠ J 5
  ♡ 9 6                │    N    │        ♡ A K J 8 3 2
  ◊ K 10 8 4          │ W     E │        ◊ 2
  ♣ A 10              │    S    │        ♣ Q 7 5 3
                       └─────────┘
                    ♠ K 8
                    ♡ Q 5 4
                    ◊ A Q 9 7 6 5 3
                    ♣ 6
```

POST MORTEM

Declarer did well to cover the ♠J because this stopped me from playing a trump next. Partner, needless to say, is the real hero. If, at the point he had laid down the ◊K, he had played a 'safe' spade, declarer would have ruffed. It would then be possible to get out for 800 either by playing a heart to cut off my hand or by leading a low diamond. Either way partner would have no safe exit after winning the fourth round of trumps.

You will note that despite my apparently modest defensive values and South's seven-card suit, we managed to collect eight tricks and a penalty worth much more than game. To pull the double, I would need a different hand, with a void in diamonds, undisclosed spade support and no ♡A, or at least two of these features. A hand like this would justify pulling:

♠ K J 5   ♡ K Q J 8 3 2   ◊ —   ♣ 8 7 5 3

One way to improve your game is to play with better or more experienced players, paying heed to what they do and listening to any useful advice they may give. Established players who helped me when I was a near rookie include Phillip Alder, Raymond Brock and Andrew Thompson. As for people who might regard me as one of their mentors, a Gold Cup winner and a Junior World champion spring to mind. If, like me, you have also done some conventional teaching, you will appreciate the thrill of hearing that one of your pupils has done something clever…

The telephone rings and one pupil, Darren, asks: 'Did you hear what Jenny did last night? She found one brilliant play. This was her hand:

♠ 10 6   ♡ A 8 4 3   ◇ A Q 10 4   ♣ 10 4 2

Jenny was in second seat and her vulnerable opponents, playing a 15-17 1NT opening, conducted a simple sequence:

WEST	NORTH	EAST	SOUTH
	pass	pass	1NT
pass	3NT	all pass	

Jenny's partner led the ♡Q and this is what she could see:

♠ K J 9
♡ 9 2
◇ J 7 5
♣ K J 9 8 5

```
        N
    W       E
        S
```

♠ 10 6
♡ A 8 4 3
◇ A Q 10 4
♣ 10 4 2

How do you think she defended?'

'Darren, you will remember that a few weeks ago we covered the importance of counting the points shown by declarer, adding those you can see and working out how many partner has from that. Jenny would therefore have added her 10 to dummy's 9 and placed her partner in the 4-6 range, of which the queen-jack of hearts she knows about.

Jenny also attended the classes in which we covered the importance of counting her opponent's tricks. If her partner has at most 3 points outside hearts, South must hold the two missing aces. With the aid of a finesse if necessary in one of the black suits, this gives declarer at least nine tricks: three spades, five clubs and the king of hearts. It would seem that the only chance of defeating the contract lies in cashing the first five tricks. Unless South has opened a skewed 1NT with a singleton king, which would show up after playing the ♡A, the only way to score five tricks quickly is to find partner with the king of diamonds. In case this card is doubleton, East should switch to the ◇4. Did Jenny do that?'

'Julian, you read Jenny's mind so well. Maybe you should be the one planning to marry her! This was the full deal:

```
                    ♠ K J 9
                    ♡ 9 2
                    ◇ J 7 5
                    ♣ K J 9 8 5
  ♠ 7 4 3 2          ┌─────────┐          ♠ 10 6
  ♡ Q J 10 7 5       │    N    │          ♡ A 8 4 3
  ◇ K 2            W │         │ E        ◇ A Q 10 4
  ♣ 7 6             │    S    │          ♣ 10 4 2
                    └─────────┘
                    ♠ A Q 8 5
                    ♡ K 6
                    ◇ 9 8 6 3
                    ♣ A Q 3
```

POST MORTEM

If West had held a third diamond, a switch to either the ace or the queen of diamonds would also have been effective. It is perhaps worth spending a few minutes examining when you might need to switch specifically to the ace or specifically to the queen.

```
              ◇ J 7 5
  ◇ 9 3 2     ┌───┐     ◇ A Q 10 4
              └───┘
              ◇ K 8 6
```

Leading the queen normally works best if you think partner does not have the king but might have an entry elsewhere. If the king takes the queen, you have a tenace over the jack; if the queen holds, you lead low next.

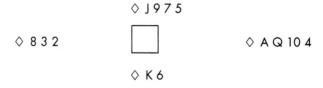

◇ J 9 7 5

◇ 8 3 2   ◇ A Q 10 4

◇ K 6

Cashing the ace is most likely to succeed if you place declarer with the king but at most one guard. Here, if you play ace and another, you can score three diamond tricks so long as partner has an entry.

Returning to the earlier theme, here are a few layouts on which you need to lead away from a strong holding.

◇ 9 7 5

◇ K 2   ◇ Q J 10 4

◇ A 8 6 3

If you need three diamond tricks and have a sure entry, it could be right to lead the four rather than the queen. This avoids a blockage when the layout is as shown.

◇ 9 7 5

◇ A 2   ◇ K Q 10 6 3

◇ J 8 4

In a suit contract it might not matter if you lead the king because partner can probably overtake with the ace and score a ruff on the third round. That option does not exist in a notrump contract. If you are looking to run the suit, you must try a low card instead, most likely the six.

Can you see the message here? Although on the opening lead you need to stick to specific methods to avoid confusing partner, you may depart from them during the play. You do so when you can tell that the 'normal' play stands little hope of success. A skilled defender relies more on counting and thinking than on rigidly adhering to convention.

Middle Route

22

Nobody can deny that the opening lead is usually the most important play on any deal. Indeed, on the examples so far, West has consistently found an effective lead. Nonetheless, there are times when a normal choice backfires and the defenders must take care not to panic or give up. This was my hand as dealer with our side vulnerable:

♠ A K J 2 ♡ A 10 3 ◇ 9 7 4 3 2 ♣ 10

In the light of my preamble you can see the case for opening 1♠. In real life, on picking up the hand in a charity pairs, I have no reason to predict that partner will be on lead and choose the normal 1◇. I can worry about a 2♣ response if and when it comes. As it happens, the need to make a rebid does not arise because South jumps to 4♡. My partner, John, passes after the customary ten-second pause following a jump bid. North takes a little longer to pass and I do so smoothly. The bidding has been:

WEST	NORTH	EAST	SOUTH
		1◇	4♡
all pass			

Partner leads the ◇Q. Dummy, despite having a void in trumps, actually looks quite good for declarer, with two ace-king combinations:

♠ 10 7 6 5 4
♡ —
◇ A K
♣ A K Q 6 3 2

	N		♠ A K J 2
W		E	♡ A 10 3
	S		◇ 9 7 4 3 2
			♣ 10

Although my play to the first trick is unimportant, it does raise a point of theory. If dummy had several trumps, there would be no future in a suit with A-K doubleton on view and my signal would be suit-preference. With dummy's actual holding but diamonds an unbid suit, one could assume that the lead of the queen promises the jack. In that case my attitude would be clear and I would signal length. As things stand, when I play the two, it ought to discourage.

Having won the diamond perforce, declarer leads the ace of clubs from dummy, on which West plays the four (standard count), and continues with the king.

With three low cards in hand, it would be strange indeed to tackle the clubs like this, considering dummy's holding. One would expect declarer to play a spade, intending to come to hand with a spade ruff and draw trumps. Surely, partner's odd number of clubs must be five rather than three.

With the threat of spade discards clear, I must ruff. The question is how high to do so. As a rule, it is wrong to ruff with the ace of trumps in such a situation. Declarer will discard a loser whilst I lose the chance to capture a high trump with my ace. Since I shall need some help from partner in the trump suit, juggling the possible holdings may tell me what to do. Can you see the way forward?

South, who appears to have no strength outside, probably has eight hearts; shapes of 2-8-2-1 and 1-8-3-1 both sound possible. Against the latter, we appear less well placed because there will be no hope of promoting a trump trick for partner on the third round of spades. I also work out that declarer, even with two losing spades, can make the contract if West has just low hearts. Although I can ruff this club and the next, we can never make more than three tricks. These will be two spades and a heart or, if declarer does not overruff, two hearts and a spade. It therefore looks like I need partner to hold at least ♡J-x. If this is the case, the idea of ruffing with the ten seems best.

In bridge, unlike chess, we do not time each player's thinking. Still, I have used up my fair share before I do ruff with the ♡10. Declarer, who has worked out that a ruff is coming, discards the ♠Q. My next play is clear — a top spade — and I am pleased to see everyone follow. When I play a second spade, declarer ruffs low before leading the king of hearts. I win with the ace and persevere with a third round of spades. Declarer ruffs with the nine, but John is no doubt happy when he overruffs with the jack to take the setting trick. This was the full deal:

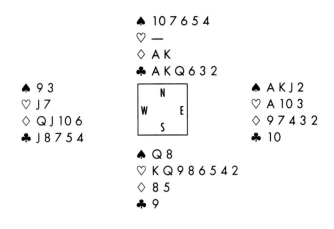

```
              ♠ 10 7 6 5 4
              ♡ —
              ◇ A K
              ♣ A K Q 6 3 2
♠ 9 3              ┌─────────┐      ♠ A K J 2
♡ J 7             │    N    │      ♡ A 10 3
◇ Q J 10 6        │ W     E │      ◇ 9 7 4 3 2
♣ J 8 7 5 4       │    S    │      ♣ 10
                   └─────────┘
              ♠ Q 8
              ♡ K Q 9 8 6 5 4 2
              ◇ 8 5
              ♣ 9
```

POST MORTEM

It would not have helped if declarer had overruffed the ♡10 with
the queen, crossed to dummy with a diamond and played a third
club. In that case, I would ruff low. Then, whether or not declarer
overruffs, I can play enough spades to give me three tricks and partner the ♡J on an overruff. Why was ruffing with the ♡10 important?

```
              ♠ 10 7 6 5 4
              ♡ —
              ◇ —
              ♣ 6 3 2
♠ 9 3              ┌─────────┐      ♠ A K J 2
♡ J 7             │    N    │      ♡ A
◇ J 10            │ W     E │      ◇ 7 4 3
♣ J 8             │    S    │      ♣ —
                   └─────────┘
              ♠ 8
              ♡ K Q 9 8 6 5 2
              ◇ —
              ♣ —
```

Were I to ruff the first club low, declarer could overruff, cross to
dummy and discard a spade when I ruff the next club with the ten.
Then, when I play two rounds of spades in the position shown,
declarer ruffs and might, reading the heart position, lead a low heart
next to avoid the promotion.

Note that ruffing with the middle card from A-10-x or similar when dummy is void usually works fine when your side needs two trump tricks. It is riskier if you need three. Give partner K-x-x of trumps for instance, and ruffing with the ten may well cost your side a trick.

Blessing in Disguise

23

At rubber bridge, if you hold a very bad hand, you normally hope that the opponents stop in a low contract to limit your losses. At duplicate, by contrast, it can be a blessing in disguise if the opponents call a slam. This may offer your only chance of a plus score. Another possibly good time to have a slam deal is when you are playing a stronger team. At IMPs and especially at aggregate scoring, a few lucky slam swings your way can more than offset other losses. On this deal from a match many moons ago, our opponents were, on paper, the stronger team. My partner, Steve, and I are playing the less endearing of their two all-male pairs in their home room. In fourth seat and with both sides vulnerable, I pick up:

♠ 9 4   ♡ J 9 3 2   ◇ 10 9 5 4   ♣ 8 5 3

Using a strong notrump and Gerber, our opponents bid as follows:

WEST	NORTH	EAST	SOUTH
			1NT
pass	4♣	pass	4♠
pass	5♣	pass	5♠
pass	7♠	all pass	

Partner leads a trump, the two, and this is what we see:

♠ K Q J 10 5 3
♡ A 7
◇ J 3
♣ A K 6

	♠ 9 4
N	♡ J 9 3 2
W E	◇ 10 9 5 4
S	♣ 8 5 3

Since declarer has shown two aces and two kings, I count him for twelve tricks: six spades, two hearts, two diamonds and two clubs. For him not to have a thirteenth, West needs both minor-suit queens and, very likely, the ♡Q as well. Partner will also need the ♣10, to prevent a successful finesse, and no more than four clubs, or declarer will be able to ruff a club in hand. The good news is that there is no sign of a claim.

Declarer wins the first spade in hand with the ace and plays one back to the king, West following, and then a third round. What do you think I can afford to discard?

If declarer has four hearts, it would be risky to discard a heart because then he could set up a long card with a ruff. Likewise, if he holds four diamonds, I need to conserve my length to prevent him from setting up one of these. This suggests discarding a club, deferring a decision on which red suit to weaken until the layout becomes clearer. Of course, this goes against the principle of guarding menaces (like the six of clubs here) on your right.

Next I spot that we may be in trouble anyway if declarer has four cards in a red suit. He can play three rounds of that suit to leave me in sole charge of it. Then, unless he holds a doubleton in the other red suit, he will also have threats in that suit and clubs. Fortunately, Steve and I lead the middle trump from three, implying that this third trump is the start of a squeeze rather than anything else. If South is 3-3-3-4, it will not matter which red suit I abandon. If he is not, the fact that he has two known high cards in diamonds and only one in hearts make 3-2-4-4 more likely than 3-4-2-4. So, I decide to discard a diamond. Reckoning that it may prove helpful to give partner a count on the suit, I begin a small echo with the ◇5.

South follows to the third trump and partner discards a low heart. On the fourth trump, I discard the ◇4 and South a low club. Partner thinks for a while, parting in the end with a diamond. On the fifth trump I wonder whether to help partner by discarding a heart, forcing him to place me with something useful in clubs, or whether to keep four hearts in case South is 3-4-3-3 but misreads the ending. For better or worse I discard the ◇9 and South discards a second club. Partner now thinks for even longer than he did before. I sit there praying that he will figure out that declarer cannot still hold three clubs. Eventually he discards a club.

On the last spade, I discard yet another diamond whilst South and West both part with clubs. The ace-king of diamonds come next and I part with two hearts. Next come the ace-king of clubs and, after following once, South discards a diamond. Presumably having worked out that this is the last diamond, partner discards the ◇Q. Three rounds of hearts complete the play, partner winning the last and setting trick with the ♡Q. This was the full deal:

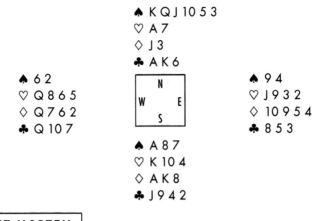

```
              ♠ K Q J 10 5 3
              ♡ A 7
              ◇ J 3
              ♣ A K 6
♠ 6 2            ┌─────┐         ♠ 9 4
♡ Q 8 6 5        │  N  │         ♡ J 9 3 2
◇ Q 7 6 2        │W   E│         ◇ 10 9 5 4
♣ Q 10 7         │  S  │         ♣ 8 5 3
                 └─────┘
              ♠ A 8 7
              ♡ K 10 4
              ◇ A K 8
              ♣ J 9 4 2
```

POST MORTEM

Although the play sounds complex, it is all down to position. East, sitting over the menace in dummy, kept clubs whilst West, sitting over declarer's red menaces, guarded those. West could cover two suits because South had to discard first and ultimately had to throw a menace. The other point is that West had to keep three clubs until South had only two left.

You may have spotted that declarer gave up the chance of a doubleton ♣Q to play for the squeeze. Against many defenders this would have worked. If East had abandoned clubs, we would have reached this ending:

```
              ♠ 10 5
              ♡ A 7
              ◇ J 3
              ♣ A K 6
♠ —             ┌─────┐         ♠ —
♡ Q 8 6         │  N  │         ♡ J 9 3 2
◇ Q 7 6         │W   E│         ◇ 10 9 5 4
♣ Q 10 7        │  S  │         ♣ 8
                └─────┘
              ♠ —
              ♡ K 10 4
              ◇ A K 8
              ♣ J 9 4
```

On the fifth spade, East discards another club, but West is in trouble. This is so even if we ignore the facts that if he throws hearts on the last two spades then the ♡10 might score on a finesse and that baring the ◇Q will set up the ◇J. The details I leave to you.

White Lie

24

What is one of the most frustrating situations you meet as a defender? Surely, it is when you can see what needs to happen to beat the contract but partner, who has to make one of the key plays, cannot. In general, there are two ways to avoid this situation. The first is to signal your holding so clearly that partner can work out the position or at any rate that an alternative will fail. The second is to tell a white lie, concealing your strength in a suit you do not want led, perhaps. One might mention a third possibility: you take control, overtaking or ruffing partner's winner.

In a local league match I am playing with my regular partner of longest standing, Graham, and pick up:

♠ Q 8 4 3   ♡ Q 10   ◇ A K Q J 10 8   ♣ 9

With nobody vulnerable, North on my right opens 1♣ in second seat. I judge that holding only two hearts makes a takeout double too great a risk. In our style, except when we hold a powerhouse, a takeout double should deliver a suitable shape as dummy for any suits partner is likely to bid. Over my 1◇, South bids 1♡ and partner passes. North rebids 1♠ and it is my turn again. If North had rebid 2♣ or 2♡, a double this time around would fit my hand perfectly. As things stand, I have the wrong shape and rebid 2◇. South bids 2♡. With our side now passing, North raises to 3♡ and South advances to game. The bidding has been:

WEST	NORTH	EAST	SOUTH
pass	1♣	1◇	1♡
pass	1♠	2◇	2♡
pass	3♡	pass	4♡
all pass			

Partner leads the ◇7 and this is what you and I see:

DEFEND THESE HANDS WITH ME

```
        ♠ A K J 2
        ♡ J 6
        ◇ 9 4
        ♣ A Q J 7 3
        ┌──────────┐
        │    N     │      ♠ Q 8 4 3
        │ W     E  │      ♡ Q 10
        │    S     │      ◇ A K Q J 10 8
        └──────────┘      ♣ 9
```

I see two diamond tricks but little scope for any in the black suits.
The club finesse, if there is one, will work. Moreover, dummy's
clubs will take care of any spade losers declarer has. In order to beat
the contract we need two trump tricks, so partner must have the ace
or king of trumps. This means that South holds 6 or 7 points and,
to justify bidding hearts twice without support and then going to
game, a seven-card heart suit.

No problem will arise if partner holds ♡A-x. I just have to cover
dummy's jack with the queen. More awkward is if he holds K-x. I
intend to play three rounds of diamonds and partner will need to
ruff the third round high. Of course, from his perspective, ruffing
would be wrong if declarer held ♡A-10-9-x-x-x; that would turn
two trump tricks into one because dummy would not have to ruff
and finesses would pick up my Q-x-x.

My singleton club gives me an idea. If I pretend to hold a void
in clubs, Graham may well decide to play the ♡K and lead a club.
Liking the sound of this, I win the first diamond with the eight
when dummy plays low. I continue with the ten and jack. Partner
can work out my holding from South's failure to beat any of my diamonds and will thus know that at each turn I am playing my lowest card. Sure enough, Graham gets the message and ruffs with the
♡K. This was the full deal:

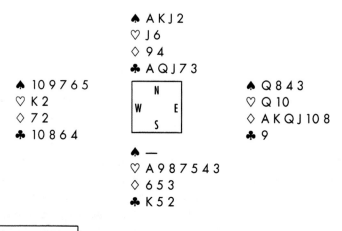

♠ A K J 2
♡ J 6
◇ 9 4
♣ A Q J 7 3

♠ 10 9 7 6 5
♡ K 2
◇ 7 2
♣ 10 8 6 4

♠ Q 8 4 3
♡ Q 10
◇ A K Q J 10 8
♣ 9

♠ —
♡ A 9 8 7 5 4 3
◇ 6 5 3
♣ K 5 2

POST MORTEM

We were slightly fortunate in that we played this deal shortly after I had read a similar problem in the *Daily Bridge Calendar*. In that problem West was posed the question of whether to ruff the third round of diamonds (after East had played normal cards) when the trump suit looked like this:

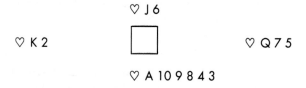

♥ J 6

♥ K 2

♥ Q 7 5

♥ A 10 9 8 4 3

On that layout, West wants to discard on the third diamond, letting dummy take the force. With the ♡J left on its own, East refuses to cover it and the king and queen both score. I could therefore anticipate the dilemma partner would face on the actual deal and was able to act accordingly.

Here are a couple of other trump layouts on which you might want to give partner the incentive or opportunity to ruff with a big trump.

♡ K 6 5

♡ A 2

♡ J 10 7

♡ Q 9 8 4 3

If declarer reads West for the ace, leading low to the king and ducking on the second round (the so-called 'obligatory finesse') will restrict the defenders to one trick. If, however, West can manage to ruff something with the ♡A, East's J-10-x becomes good for a trick and the defenders make two trump tricks instead of one.

This position is similar, although now declarer is almost certain to play the suit in a way to hold the defenders to two trump tricks. If they want to get three, arranging for West to ruff something with the ♡A is a good way to go about it. Can you see why ruffing gains a trick in these two layouts and in the one in the main text? West scores a trick with a master trump that would not, if it had been played on a trump trick, have captured a high card from declarer (or dummy).

Communication Corridor

25

Sometimes as a defender, you can tell that you stand no chance of beating the contract (your normal goal at IMPs or any form of aggregate scoring), if declarer holds a particular card. In this case, you will, if it is possible on the bidding and play to date, place your partner with the card in question. You can then go on to place other missing cards on the basis that your initial assumption will prove correct.

In a match between Cambridge University and one of the nearby county sides, you see me pick up the following hand:

♠ K Q 10 9 5   ♡ Q 4   ◇ K 2   ♣ J 10 6 3

Our side is vulnerable and the gentleman on my right opens 1◇. With a strong five-card suit, roughly opening values and the chance to bid at the one-level, I have an easy bid: 1♠. The lady on my left jumps to 2NT and Richard, my partner, passes. North's raise to 3NT ends the bidding:

WEST	NORTH	EAST	SOUTH
	1◇	1♠	2NT
pass	3NT	all pass	

Partner leads the ♠7 and we can now see these hands:

```
              ♠ 6 3
              ♡ K 8 6
              ◇ Q J 10 8 7 3
              ♣ A K
           ┌─────────┐
           │    N    │      ♠ K Q 10 9 5
           │ W     E │      ♡ Q 4
           │    S    │      ◇ K 2
           └─────────┘      ♣ J 10 6 3
```

In our methods the ♠7 probably comes from ♠7-x. Other possibilities include ♠8-7-x, a singleton seven and, if South has taken a bit of a flier, ♠J-8-7. Leading low from x-x-x if partner has bid a suit that you have not supported has yet to catch on in Europe and was very uncommon in 1983.

The thing that most strikes me having seen the dummy is that we stand no real chance of beating the contract unless partner has the ◇A. If the diamonds are solid, declarer must have a minimum of nine tricks. Giving Richard the ◇A means we have two diamond winners/entries/stoppers and this should give us time to set up some tricks of our own.

The snag is that if I play the ♠Q and it holds, we will only be able to set up the spades if partner has three spades. Since declarer surely has two spade stoppers, it makes sense to play the ♠9 instead.

I do play the ♠9 and it wins. Assuming declarer would not be so brave (or foolish) to duck with A-J-x, the spade suit is probably now dead. If I switch, it seems a close call whether to play a club or a heart. In clubs, partner needs only the queen but, in hearts, he will need the J-9 or J-10. An inspection of the opponents' convention card reveals that they play negative doubles. This reduces the chance that South has four hearts and tips the odds towards leading a heart.

I lead the ♡Q and declarer plays low. Partner encourages with the ♡7 and the king wins. The ◇Q comes next, with these cards visible:

```
        ♠ 6
        ♡ 8 6
        ◇ Q J 10 8 7 3
        ♣ A K
     ┌─────────┐
     │    N    │         ♠ K Q 10 5
     │ W     E │         ♡ 4
     │    S    │         ◇ K 2
     └─────────┘         ♣ J 10 6 3
```

If partner's opening lead came from J-8-7, I should let him win the first diamond and revert to spades. In practice, his play of the ♡7 must surely make setting up the hearts a better bet. Therefore, I play the ◇K and, when this holds, lead the ♡4. Declarer plays the ♡10 but partner wins with the jack and plays a third round. I discard a low spade and the ♡A wins. A second round of diamonds goes to partner's ace and he proceeds to cash two long hearts to defeat the contract. 'Not my day,' grumbles South as we all inspect the full deal:

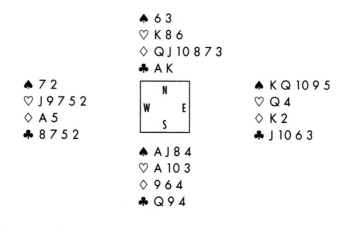

```
            ♠ 6 3
            ♡ K 8 6
            ◇ Q J 10 8 7 3
            ♣ A K
♠ 7 2                          ♠ K Q 10 9 5
♡ J 9 7 5 2     N              ♡ Q 4
◇ A 5        W     E           ◇ K 2
♣ 8 7 5 2       S              ♣ J 10 6 3
            ♠ A J 8 4
            ♡ A 10 3
            ◇ 9 6 4
            ♣ Q 9 4
```

POST MORTEM

Clearly, the contract fails if declarer wins the first trick; West will win the first diamond and continue spades. Note also that it does not help to duck the ♡Q; East will revert to spades and we score two spades, a heart and two diamonds. Ducking the ♡Q would have worked, though, if East had played the ♠Q at Trick 1; then we cannot win any more spade tricks.

If partner leads from a doubleton against a notrump contract, it often pays not to play high, thereby forcing declarer to use a stopper at once. In the first layout below, you can run the spades if you duck the first spade and partner has an entry. In the second and third, you can run the suit if both defenders have an entry and West gets in first.

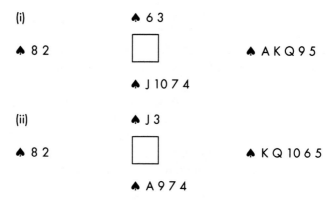

```
(i)              ♠ 6 3

♠ 8 2                          ♠ A K Q 9 5

                 ♠ J 10 7 4

(ii)             ♠ J 3

♠ 8 2                          ♠ K Q 10 6 5

                 ♠ A 9 7 4
```

(iii)

♠ 83

♠ 92      ♠ K Q 10 6 5 4

♠ A J 7

As a defender, you have quite a few signals available to request the lead of a particular suit. If partner has led it, you can encourage. If you are making a discard, you can either ask for that suit or discourage another suit. If you are delivering a ruff or have already given a primary signal when following suit, you can give a suit-preference signal. Unfortunately, sometimes none of these options is available and you have to choose a sequence of plays to put partner on the right track.

♠ K 10 7 2   ♡ J 9   ◊ A Q 4   ♣ A J 7 6

As dealer at rubber bridge with both sides vulnerable, I pick up this hand and open a strong 1NT. The flamboyantly dressed gentleman on my left overcalls 2♡ and my more modestly attired partner passes. The lady on my right slowly raises to 3♡ and this ends the auction:

WEST	NORTH	EAST	SOUTH
		1NT	2♡
pass	3♡	all pass	

Partner leads the ◊2 and we see that North had a choice of bids over her partner's 2♡. What would you have bid? An expert panel would probably award votes to 3♡, 2NT, 3◊ and possibly to other actions as well.

♠ Q 8 3
♡ K Q
◊ K J 10 7 6 5
♣ Q 5

```
          N
      W        E        ♠ K 10 7 2
          S             ♡ J 9
                        ◊ A Q 4
                        ♣ A J 7 6
```

For once, one can almost write down the unseen hands at Trick 1. Seeing all the top five diamonds, I can read the lead as a singleton. South, to come in over a strong 1NT when vulnerable, surely holds the two missing aces, the ♣K and a six-card heart suit. (With seven hearts, he would have accepted North's game invitation).

Making four tricks looks easy enough — the ace-queen of diamonds, a ruff and the ♣A. In order to beat the contract we need a spade trick as well, which means partner will need the ♠J.

It is not hard to spot that starting with three rounds of diamonds will fail. Having ruffed, partner will have only two trumps left. This will put declarer in a position to draw trumps ending in dummy and run the diamonds. We will need to cash the ♣A merely to prevent an overtrick.

I shall need to give partner his diamond ruff on the second round of the suit, leaving myself with a stopper. My next problem comes from trying to get him to lead a spade after that rather than a club.

My diamond plays are both forced: winning the first trick cheaply and returning the four for partner to ruff. Is there anything else I can do?

It strikes me that if declarer has six hearts, three diamonds and a high card in each black suit, his most likely shape is 2-6-3-2. Anyway, we can never beat the contract if South has a singleton ♠A. If he is 2-6-3-2, I can afford to cash the ♣A before giving partner a ruff. Can this help?

In a high-standard game, it is fairly common to play that after the first trick you should lead the king from ace-king. The thinking behind this it is much easier for either defender to judge when the lead of an unsupported ace is safe once you have seen the dummy. Also, one of the defenders, the opening leader, is most unlikely to hold an ace-king combination and not lead it initially. I hope therefore that cashing the ♣A will tell him that there is no future in the club suit and direct his attention to spades.

Alas, the message does not get through. Partner ruffs the second round of diamonds and returns a club. Declarer overtakes the queen with the king, draws one round of trumps and leads a diamond. When I win perforce and lead a low spade, declarer lets this run round to dummy's queen and claims the contract. This was the full deal:

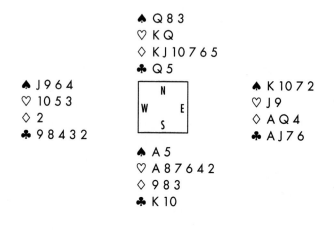

```
              ♠ Q 8 3
              ♡ K Q
              ◇ K J 10 7 6 5
              ♣ Q 5
♠ J 9 6 4         N         ♠ K 10 7 2
♡ 10 5 3      W       E     ♡ J 9
◇ 2               S         ◇ A Q 4
♣ 9 8 4 3 2                 ♣ A J 7 6
              ♠ A 5
              ♡ A 8 7 6 4 2
              ◇ 9 8 3
              ♣ K 10
```

POST MORTEM

'Sorry, I thought you cashed the ace of clubs because you wanted a club back,' partner says apologetically.

'Yes, it was difficult for you,' I reply. 'I was hoping you'd work out that with both top clubs I would cash the king rather than ace. With the queen on view in dummy it would be obvious who holds the ace if the king wins the trick. In addition, with both top clubs, there were two other things I could have done. For one thing, since we could only ever take one ruff, I could have simply cashed both top clubs before letting you have the ruff. For another, if all my winners were quick ones, it would not have been necessary to play the low diamond back. It would have been safe to cash both diamond winners before giving you the ruff.'

'Weren't you taking a slight chance when you cashed the ace of clubs that declarer might have a singleton ♣K? In that case, couldn't he win the spade switch you wanted me to make in his hand, cross to dummy with a trump and discard his remaining diamond on the ♣Q?'

'Yes, if South is 3-6-3-1, I need to give you the ruff straight away and pray that you will find the spade switch. Since the odds looked to be at least 50-50 that you would lead a club after taking your ruff, it seemed worth taking that chance to point you in the right direction. I agree that this is a tough play to find, especially in an irregular partnership.

Short-Lived Pleasure

As a defender, you try to avoid playing high cards that might be ruffed if doing so will set up a winner in dummy. What are the exceptions to this? You will be safe if dummy has no entries, declarer's only losers are in trumps or are fast ones, or if partner can ruff dummy's newly established winner. Indeed, suppose that playing top cards has already set up a winner in dummy and you know that only you and dummy have cards left in the suit. In this case, you may try to play the suit again before trumps are drawn so that partner can ruff to stop declarer from taking a discard.

In a local league match I am in fourth seat and pick up the following hand when neither side is vulnerable:

♠ A 7   ♡ A 8 7 2   ◊ Q 9 8 2   ♣ Q 7 3

South opens a weak 2♠ and, after West passes, North bids 3♠. This preemptive raise leaves the level too high for me and ends the auction:

WEST	NORTH	EAST	SOUTH
			2♠
pass	3♠	all pass	

Partner leads the ◊A and these cards are in my view:

    ♠ K J 3
    ♡ K 9
    ◊ J 10 6 3
    ♣ K 9 6 4

	N		♠ A 7
W		E	♡ A 8 7 2
	S		◊ Q 9 8 2
			♣ Q 7 3

My first priority is to decide whether to ask for a diamond continuation. I fear that South has a singleton and partner will play the ◊K next, setting up a ruffing finesse. With the ten of hearts as well as the ace it would be clear to discourage because a heart switch, partner's most likely action, could not cost. As things stand, I wish that we were playing count signals and could transfer the problem across the table. Since playing the nine slowly might cause partner an ethical problem, I elect to play the two.

Partner switches to the ♡J and dummy plays low. What do you think I should do?

Since we can make only two tricks in the majors with my two aces, we will need three in the minors. If South started with a singleton diamond, we will need three club tricks (or two clubs and a ruff). I soon conclude that we are unlikely to get them. With the club ace, partner would have 12 or 13 points, presumably enough for a takeout double of 2♠. Without it, South would have only 4 or 5 points, probably a little light for opening on a queen-high suit at equal vulnerability. On this basis, it seems right to assume that a second diamond will stand up and to focus on securing the setting trick. This surely has to come from a third-round club winner.

I could put up the ♡A and shift to a club, playing partner for ♣J-10-x. Do you think there might be a way to beat the contract when it is South who holds the ♣10? My ♠A means that declarer cannot draw trumps quickly and gives me the option to wipe out any danger that a fourth-round winner in dummy will provide a discard. I put up the ♡A, lead the ◇Q, pleased to see that all follow, and lead a third round of diamonds. Ruffing this, declarer plays a trump to the king. These are the cards left visible:

```
              ♠ K J 3
              ♡ K
              ◇ J
              ♣ K 9 6 4
         ┌──────────┐
         │    N     │        ♠ A 7
         │ W      E │        ♡ 8 7 2
         │    S     │        ◇ 8
         └──────────┘        ♣ Q 7 3
```

I must take the ace now, to play a fourth round of diamonds while partner still has a trump left. When declarer starts thinking, it becomes clear that the contract is going down. If he were looking at ♣A-J-x, it would be obvious for him to ruff the diamond and rely on the club finesse rather than to play me for both missing trumps. When South throws a club, West ruffs, the full deal being:

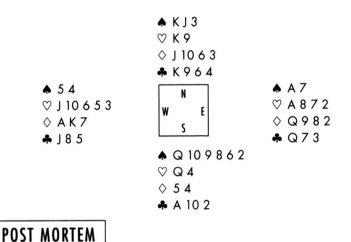

```
              ♠ K J 3
              ♡ K 9
              ◇ J 10 6 3
              ♣ K 9 6 4
  ♠ 5 4          ┌─────┐         ♠ A 7
  ♡ J 10 6 5 3   │  N  │         ♡ A 8 7 2
  ◇ A K 7        │W   E│         ◇ Q 9 8 2
  ♣ J 8 5        │  S  │         ♣ Q 7 3
                 └─────┘
              ♠ Q 10 9 8 6 2
              ♡ Q 4
              ◇ 5 4
              ♣ A 10 2
```

POST MORTEM

You may have noticed that, when switching back to diamonds, I led
the queen. I did this to make sure partner would not get any silly
ideas, taking the ◇K and leading a club through dummy's king for
example. It was important to get in four rounds of diamonds before
trumps were drawn. The same would apply if we make a few
tweaks to the deal, like this:

```
              ♠ K J 3
              ♡ K 9
              ◇ Q J 6 3
              ♣ K 9 6 4
  ♠ 5 4            ┌─────┐       ♠ A 7
  ♡ A J 10 6 5 3   │  N  │       ♡ 8 7 2
  ◇ 8 7            │W   E│       ◇ A K 9 4 2
  ♣ Q 8 5          │  S  │       ♣ J 7 3
                   └─────┘
              ♠ Q 10 9 8 6 2
              ♡ Q 4
              ◇ 10 5
              ♣ A 10 2
```

Once more, South plays in 3♠ after opening a weak 2♠; West leads
a diamond, the eight this time. In order to defeat the contract, East
must cash two diamonds and play a third round. Declarer cannot
afford to let West score a lowly trump and ruffs high. The first
round of trumps goes to East's ace and a fourth diamond gives
declarer a familiar and unhappy choice: discard a club in the hope
West began with a singleton trump or ruff in the even fainter hope
of playing the clubs for no loser.

Chicago has become the popular format for cut-in bridge in homes and clubs in North America and is now taking over at the top London clubs. As its other name, four-deal bridge, implies, each 'rubber' (or 'pivot' as you may hear it called) consists of exactly four deals. This spares the risk of a long delay if you are waiting for a traditional rubber to finish, either if you are sitting out or you do not see eye to eye with your partner! The way most people play, you can still carry forward partscores, although the limited time in which to convert them to game reduces their value. You can play that the non-dealing side is vulnerable on the second and third deals of a 'rubber'. We have that agreement when I pick up:

♠ Q 9 7 2   ♡ A   ◊ 10 9 3   ♣ A J 9 5 4

Partner deals and opens 4♡. Two passes follow and South, a bearded gentleman, bids 5◊. Although I expect to beat this more often than not, for me that is not a good enough reason to double. The bidding has been:

WEST	NORTH	EAST	SOUTH
4♡	pass	pass	5◊
all pass			

Partner leads the ♡K and this modest dummy raises defensive hopes:

```
              ♠ J 10 8 6
              ♡ 7 6
              ◊ 7 2
              ♣ K Q 7 6 2
         ┌──────────┐
         │    N     │      ♠ Q 9 7 2
         │ W      E │      ♡ A
         │    S     │      ◊ 10 9 3
         └──────────┘      ♣ A J 9 5 4
```

When declarer plays low from dummy quickly, it would be possible to say 'I am thinking about the deal as a whole' and pause to reflect now. It seems easier in unfamiliar company, however, to take my ace smoothly and take my time before leading to the next trick.

One cannot say for certain, but partner might have led a single-ton club. This persuades me to place declarer with a singleton or perhaps a void in clubs. In this case declarer's diamonds are probably very good because, if not, he could have doubled 4♡, a more flexible action. He would then have been able to defend 4♡ doubled, pass 4♠ or convert 5♣ to 5◇.

If partner has the ace or king of spades, then any normal play will beat the contract. The task appears harder if, as I intend to assume, South has the two top spades. These are some typical hands for him:

♠ A K 3	♠ A K 3	♠ A K 3
♡ 8 4	♡ 8	♡ 8 4
◇ A K Q J 8 6 5 4	◇ A K Q J 8 6 5 4	◇ A K Q J 8 6 5
♣ —	♣ 8	♣ 8

If he holds the first hand, there is no need to do anything special. I can just shift passively to the ◇10. If he wins and runs an avalanche of trumps, I simply need to keep my queen of spades guarded and the ♣A.

Unfortunately, if he holds the second hand, a diamond switch will not work. Declarer will win, draw trumps, perhaps taking a few extra rounds 'for lurkers' and play a club. After taking my ♣A, I shall have to return a spade, which will run round to dummy's jack for his eleventh trick. A very similar problem will arise if he holds the third hand, which surely sounds the most likely of the three because it means that the missing diamonds are 7-1 rather than 8-0. After scoring my ♣A, again I shall have to play a spade. This time the ♠J provides not just a trick but also an entry to dummy's club winner, letting declarer discard a losing heart.

The fact that the problem on the second and third layouts arises when I come in with the ♣A after my exit cards in trumps have gone suggests a solution. What do you think of cashing the ♣A before doing anything else? If, as seems likely, South has a single-ton club, this will cut him off from dummy. I shall also have the option of playing a second round if partner's card does not look consistent with a doubleton. In fact, partner plays the ten and I carry through with my plan, leading the ◇10 next.

Declarer wins the diamond, West following, and runs all his trumps. Luckily for us, this presents no problem. His failure to claim confirms that he has no more clubs and I hang on to my spades, scoring the ♠Q on the last trick. This was the full deal:

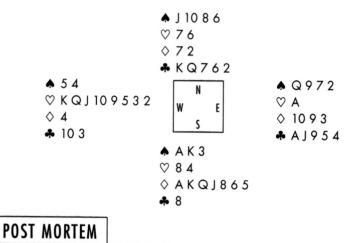

```
                    ♠ J 10 8 6
                    ♡ 7 6
                    ◊ 7 2
                    ♣ K Q 7 6 2
  ♠ 5 4                               ♠ Q 9 7 2
  ♡ K Q J 10 9 5 3 2      N           ♡ A
  ◊ 4                  W     E        ◊ 10 9 3
  ♣ 10 3                  S           ♣ A J 9 5 4
                    ♠ A K 3
                    ♡ 8 4
                    ◊ A K Q J 8 6 5
                    ♣ 8
```

POST MORTEM

Since cashing the ♣A could have backfired if South held a double-ton club and I did not play a second round, you might wonder whether it would have been good enough for me instead to return a spade at Trick 2. If declarer carelessly lets the lead run round to dummy then the answer is yes; I would hang on to all my spades to leave myself with an exit card. Suppose, however, that declarer wins the spade in hand, draws trumps and plays a club. Then, in the position shown below, I will be stuck.

```
                    ♠ J 10 8
                    ♡ —
                    ◊ —
                    ♣ K Q
  ♠ 4                               ♠ Q 9 7
  ♡ J 10                  N           ♡ —
  ◊ —                  W     E        ◊ —
  ♣ 10 3                  S           ♣ A J
                    ♠ K 3
                    ♡ 4
                    ◊ 5
                    ♣ 8
```

After taking my ♣A, I can do nothing to stop dummy from making tricks in both spades and clubs.

Sometimes, indeed quite often, the defenders need to attack a specific suit but only one of them can do so safely or at all. If partner needs to play the suit, you might unblock your high cards elsewhere or underlead a winner. If you need to play it, you might step in smartly with a high card or even overtake or ruff one of partner's winners.

Playing with my mother, Pam, in a tournament over the Easter festival, I pick up the following hand as dealer with both sides vulnerable:

♠ A Q ♡ 7 6 3 2 ◇ A Q 9 7 2 ♣ 10 6

With all my strength in two suits and a non-classical shape for 1NT, I open 1◇. The young man on my left overcalls 1♡, and partner bids 1♠, showing a five-card suit. The slightly older man on my right bids 1NT. With a minimum opening, I pass and South's jump to 4♡ ends the auction:

WEST	NORTH	EAST	SOUTH
		1◇	1♡
1♠	1NT	pass	4♡
all pass			

Partner leads the ◇J and dummy comes down as follows:

```
        ♠ J 9 5 4
        ♡ Q 10
        ◇ K 8 6 4
        ♣ A 8 3
      ┌──────────┐      ♠ A Q
      │    N     │      ♡ 7 6 3 2
      │ W     E  │      ◇ A Q 9 7 2
      │    S     │      ♣ 10 6
      └──────────┘
```

Declarer, to jump to 4♡ with no support from his partner, very likely holds a seven-card heart suit. He also needs something on the side, one of the black kings, no doubt. With a 2-7-2-2 shape and no ♠K, he must lose two spades and two diamonds, whilst game must be cold if he has ♣K-Q-x. Here are some hands for him on which my play might matter:

♠ K 2	♠ K 2	♠ 7 2
♡ A K J 9 8 5 4	♡ A K J 9 8 5 4	♡ A K J 9 8 5 4
◇ 5 3	◇ 5	◇ 5
♣ Q 4	♣ Q 7 4	♣ K J 4

If he holds the first hand, we do not need to do anything special. I simply need to play a club to knock out the ace while I still have trumps left. This will ensure that declarer cannot discard a loser on the ♠J. It will not be difficult for me because I have more trumps than dummy and the only way he can reach dummy to play a spade up to his king is in trumps.

The position is similar if he holds the second hand. I can wait to come in with the ♠A and then shift to the ♣10, hoping that declarer's middle club is the seven or lower, as shown. In this case, he can hold up for one round, but it does him no good because a club continuation will kill dummy's entry.

The third hand, which seems the most likely of the three, presents a problem. Although taking the club finesse would fail, declarer must have other chances. He will find out about my heart length and, since I would have opened 1NT with a 2-4-4-3 shape, he may well guess my shape. If he does place me with two clubs, he will not take the club finesse (and his clubs might be just K-9-x, in which case he would not have the option). The thing that worries me is a squeeze on partner in the black suits.

Suppose we start with the jack and ten of diamonds, and declarer discards a spade on the second round. He can then give up one spade and ruff another. This will establish the spade threat against partner. I cannot knock out dummy's ♣A entry because I get in only once in spades and he can win my club switch in hand with the king. I can afford to let the ◇J hold but if, as indeed she does, partner continues with the ◇10, it is vital to overtake with the queen. If declarer discards a spade now, I can switch to a club. In practice, he ruffs. He then crosses to dummy with a trump, partner discarding the ♠3, and calls for a spade. We play count discards, which means declarer cannot have a singleton ♠K, and I play the queen to make sure partner cannot go wrong. This wins and I lead the ♣10. South wins with the ♣K and rattles off all his trumps.

I have no problem with my discards. For the last three tricks, I keep my two aces and a club. Although partner has more difficulty, she does the right thing. Her next four discards are two low clubs, a diamond and a spade. Then, on the last trump, when clearly she has ♣Q-9 and ♠K-x left, she bares the ♠K. Finally, declarer crosses to the ♣A and, when the queen does not fall, concedes one down. This was the full deal:

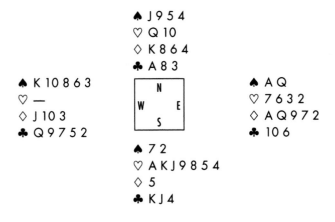

              ♠ J 9 5 4
              ♡ Q 10
              ◇ K 8 6 4
              ♣ A 8 3

♠ K 10 8 6 3   ♠ A Q
♡ —   ♡ 7 6 3 2
◇ J 10 3   ◇ A Q 9 7 2
♣ Q 9 7 5 2   ♣ 10 6

              ♠ 7 2
              ♡ A K J 9 8 5 4
              ◇ 5
              ♣ K J 4

POST MORTEM

Declarer probably did the right thing in running the trumps without giving up a second spade to rectify the count. With this line, we had to take care. If I had parted with my second club, allowing declarer to give up a spade, or if I had allowed him to give up a diamond to partner, the ending could have been like this:

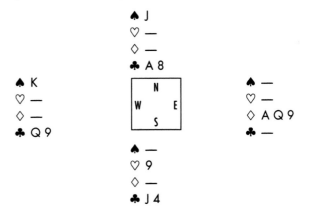

              ♠ J
              ♡ —
              ◇ —
              ♣ A 8

♠ K   ♠ —
♡ —   ♡ —
◇ —   ◇ A Q 9
♣ Q 9   ♣ —

              ♠ —
              ♡ 9
              ◇ —
              ♣ J 4

West has no safe discard on the last trump.

Inspired Lead 30

The Pachabo, in which the champion teams from each county of England compete, has an unusual scoring method. In each three-board match, two victory points are available per board to the team that wins it or, if there is no swing (or a difference of only 10), they score one each. Four more victory points come from comparing the total aggregate scores for each side on the three boards. The idea, it seems, is to make every board count for something whilst encouraging people to play 'normal' bridge.

At dinner on the first day of the event, our team is waiting for our order to arrive and are discussing the interesting deals. 'What happened at your table on board 30?' Graham, my partner, asks of our teammates. 'We collected 300 against 1NT doubled and we were hoping to win the board. 3NT was hopeless our way and we thought 4♠ would go down on a trump lead.'

'Board 30, you say,' replies David, one of our teammates scanning his scorecard. 'Ah, yes, our opponents played in 4♠ from the South seat and I led a trump. I had very little and couldn't do anything.'

'Maybe I screwed up,' says Steve, David's partner. 'This was my hand:

♠ 10 9 6   ♡ A K 10 2   ◇ 9 2   ♣ A J 9 6

Since we play a strong notrump, I opened 1♣. After the player on my left bid 1♠, David passed and the player on my right bid 2♣. This was a value raise or unassuming cuebid, whatever you want to call it. South tried to sign off in 2♠ but North jumped to 4♠. This was the auction:

WEST	NORTH	EAST	SOUTH
		1♣	1♠
pass	2♣	pass	2♠
pass	4♠	all pass	

When dummy came down, this is what I could see,' Steve continues, covering up the West and South hands on the printout of the deal:

```
        ♠ K 7 4
        ♡ Q J
        ◇ A Q 6 4
        ♣ K Q 10 2
    ┌─────────┐      ♠ 10 9 6
    │    N    │      ♡ A K 10 2
    │ W     E │      ◇ 9 2
    │    S    │      ♣ A J 9 6
    └─────────┘
```

Declarer won the opening lead in hand with the ace of trumps and led a heart. I won with the king and returned a trump. Declarer won in hand with the queen, David following, and played a club this time. David played the three, standard count, and I captured dummy's king with my ace to play a third round of trumps. Partner discarded a low heart and dummy's king won.' Steve looks questioningly at his partner. 'What happened after that?'

'Declarer came to hand with the ◇K,' David says, 'and played a fourth round of trumps. I threw a heart, dummy the ♡Q and you a heart as well.'

'I've got it now,' Steve resumes. 'A diamond went to the ace and then came the ◇Q. With dummy entryless apart from clubs, I could afford to throw a club. Then, knowing David still had a diamond left, declarer ruffed a diamond in hand. I threw a heart. Was that the right thing to do?'

```
        ♠ —
        ♡ —
        ◇ 6
        ♣ Q 10 2
    ┌─────────┐      ♠ —
    │    N    │      ♡ A 10
    │ W     E │      ◇ —
    │    S    │      ♣ J 9
    └─────────┘
```

'I was expecting a losing finesse of the ♣10 into my jack. Instead, the declarer exited with a heart. I made my ace but then had to lead a club.

'It might have been better to discard a club. Then declarer would have had to guess which of us held the club jack,' David replies. 'I think I did my best in keeping both my remaining clubs.'

'True,' Graham adds, 'but Steve would have only 11 points without the club jack. I wonder if you had a way to avoid this ending. What was the full deal?'

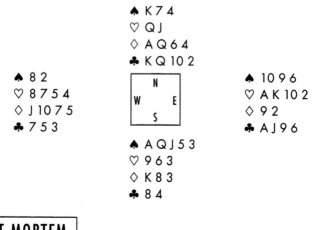

```
                    ♠ K 7 4
                    ♡ Q J
                    ◇ A Q 6 4
                    ♣ K Q 10 2
   ♠ 8 2                              ♠ 10 9 6
   ♡ 8 7 5 4          N               ♡ A K 10 2
   ◇ J 10 7 5     W       E           ◇ 9 2
   ♣ 7 5 3             S               ♣ A J 9 6
                    ♠ A Q J 5 3
                    ♡ 9 6 3
                    ◇ K 8 3
                    ♣ 8 4
```

POST MORTEM

'There was a way to beat the contract,' I observe. 'Steve didn't need to win the first club to play a trump. Declarer couldn't take ruffs without giving up a heart, and you had the master heart and the third trump. So, after your ♣6, suppose that declarer left the hearts alone, drawing trumps and testing the diamonds as before. This would have been the ending:

```
                    ♠ —
                    ♡ —
                    ◇ 6
                    ♣ Q 10 2
   ♠ —                                ♠ —
   ♡ 8              N                  ♡ A 10
   ◇ J           W     E               ◇ —
   ♣ 7 5             S                 ♣ A J
                    ♠ 5
                    ♡ 9 6
                    ◇ —
                    ♣ 8
```

Now you, rather than dummy, have the major tenace in clubs. You're not in any difficulty on the fourth round of diamonds. You simply discard the ♣J, leaving yourself with all winners. In practice, the position would not arise. Declarer would try for a heart ruff or the finesse in clubs.'

On many deals, the choice of opening lead is critical. If you can attack declarer's weak spot, you are off to a good start. Nonetheless, you must take care not to rest on your laurels. For one thing, you may not have hit your opponent's very weakest spot. For another, until you take the setting trick, you must beware of what might happen in the endgame.

As West now, with only the opponents vulnerable, I pick up:

♠ A 9 2   ♡ K J 8 7 6 3 ◇ K 5 ♣ 7 3

South, the dealer, opens a strong 1NT and I overcall 2♡. North bids 4♡, alerted and explained as a Texas transfer showing spades, and partner doubles. South completes the transfer with 4♠ to end the bidding:

WEST	NORTH	EAST	SOUTH
			1NT
2♡	4♡	dbl	4♠
all pass			

East's double asks for a heart lead and must show the ace. After toying with leading the ♡8 as a suit-preference signal for diamonds, I decide that is a bit deep and settle for a fourth-best ♡7. This is what we see:

♠ K Q 10 7 6 5
♡ 9 5
◇ 6 4
♣ Q J 9

♠ A 9 2
♡ K J 8 7 6 3
◇ K 5
♣ 7 3

```
      N
  W       E
      S
```

Partner wins with the ♡A and returns the two. South, who played low on the first round, puts up the queen and my king wins. Since with A-10-2 it would be normal for partner to return the ten, declarer, whose name is Conrad, must have the missing heart. This makes it an easy decision to play a third round of hearts. Dummy ruffs with the ten and partner discards the ◇3.

Declarer leads the ♣9 off dummy and, after partner plays the six, wins with the ace. He leads a low trump next, the four to be precise. Had he ruffed the third round of hearts with dummy's king or queen, I would feel tempted now to go in with the ace and play a fourth round of hearts in the hope partner had the ♠J and could overruff. As things stand, I choose to duck, making declarer's communications with dummy difficult and maybe giving me the chance to see a further discard from partner. The king wins this first round of trumps, partner following with the three. A low trump then goes to the eight, jack and ace. What do you suggest leading next?

```
              ♠ Q 7 6
              ♡ —
              ◇ 6 4
              ♣ Q J
  ♠ 9              ┌─────────┐
  ♡ 8 6 3          │    N    │
  ◇ K 5            │ W     E │
  ♣ 3              │    S    │
                   └─────────┘
```

South started with 15-17 points and, so far, we have seen the ♣A, the ♡Q and the ♠J. To make up his total he will need the ◇A, the ♣K and one or both of the ◇J and ◇Q. If he started with a 2-3-5-3 shape, then exiting safely with a black card will defeat the contract even if he holds all the missing high cards. Two clues, however, point to a 2-3-4-4 shape. Firstly, partner, holding five clubs and four diamonds, might well have discarded a club rather than a diamond on the third round of hearts. Secondly, and more significantly perhaps, partner's ♣6 on the first round of clubs looks like the start of a high-low from ♣10-6-x-x or ♣8-6-x-x.

If declarer began with ♣A-K-10-x, we cannot stop him from using the ♣Q as an entry to draw the last trump, then overtaking the third round of clubs and throwing dummy's losing diamond on the ♣10. We must hope he does not have that ♣10, in which case the clubs will be blocked. Since at present he has the ◇A as a re-entry to overcome the blockage, I must lead a diamond to knock it out, playing partner for the ◇Q. The standard lead from a doubleton is high. Here there seems to be a good case for making an exception.

Declarer, after taking my diamond switch with the ace, will surely cross to the ♣Q to draw the last trump. He may well run the rest of the trumps and partner, trying to keep the ◇Q and the clubs, will be squeezed. So, I lead the ◇5. Partner puts up the queen and declarer takes the line I predicted: the squeeze would still have worked if East had ◇K-Q, but it is not to be. For the last trick, I have the ◇K, East the ♣10 and it does not matter whether South keeps the ♣8 or ◇J. This was the full deal:

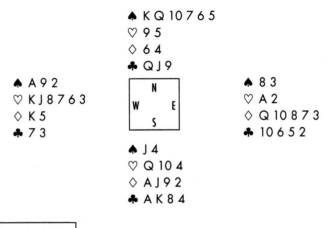

```
                    ♠ K Q 10 7 6 5
                    ♡ 9 5
                    ◇ 6 4
                    ♣ Q J 9
  ♠ A 9 2                            ♠ 8 3
  ♡ K J 8 7 6 3      N              ♡ A 2
  ◇ K 5          W       E          ◇ Q 10 8 7 3
  ♣ 7 3              S              ♣ 10 6 5 2
                    ♠ J 4
                    ♡ Q 10 4
                    ◇ A J 9 2
                    ♣ A K 8 4
```

POST MORTEM

Obviously, we could beat the contract by leading diamonds earlier. As it was, the danger that I might capture a high trump with my ace and play a fourth heart forced declarer to block the clubs. Once he did that, it was vital to use East's ◇Q to knock out his ◇A. If I had wasted my ◇K, we would have reached this simple squeeze ending, with dummy on lead:

```
                    ♠ 6
                    ♡ —
                    ◇ 6
                    ♣ J
  ♠ —                               ♠ —
  ♡ 8 6              N              ♡ —
  ◇ 5            W       E          ◇ Q
  ♣ —                S              ♣ 10 5
                    ♠ —
                    ♡ —
                    ◇ J
                    ♣ K 8
```

All Bases Covered

As declarer, you often have two chances to succeed, a winning finesse or an even break, for example. As a counter, the defenders will aim to force you to take the finesse before you can test for the even break. Another example of having two strings to your bow is being able either to ruff losers in dummy or throw them on dummy's winners. This can be harder to counter: leading trumps deals with the first string but not the second.

♠ 7 6 4 3   ♡ Q 10 7   ◇ A K J 9   ♣ A 3

In the teams event of a National tournament, I pick up this hand with our side vulnerable and, playing a strong notrump, open 1◇. The next hand overcalls 1♡ and David, my partner, makes a negative double, showing four spades. The next hand, South, bids 2♣ and I bid 2♠. After two passes, South reopens with a competitive double. North removes this to 3♣, which becomes the final contract. The bidding has been:

WEST	NORTH	EAST	SOUTH
1◇	1♡	dbl	2♣
2♠	pass	pass	dbl
pass	3♣	all pass	

I lead the ◇A and see this dummy:

♠ A J 10 2
♡ K 8 6 5 2
◇ 7 2
♣ Q 4

♠ 7 6 4 3   [N]
♡ Q 10 7   W   E
◇ A K J 9   [S]
♣ A 3

Partner follows with the ◇3 and South with the four. I am still on lead.

It occurs to me that the declarer, a distinguished gentleman, figures to be 1-2-4-6. If South had no spades or fewer diamonds, my

partner might have bid on; also, with seven clubs, he might have bid
3♣ rather than doubling. Where do you think the high cards are?
There are 16 points out and the bidding marks East with 5 or 6 and
South with 10 or 11. If declarer's spade is a low one, partner will hold
the ♠K-Q and South most, if not all, of the other high cards.

Cashing the ◊K is out because that may well set up declarer's
queen. I also exclude ace and another trump. Declarer could probably play a heart to the ace, draw the last trump and establish the hearts
by ruffing. It looks better to shift to a spade. If the ace goes up and
declarer tries a diamond, I can play ace and another trump, knowing
there is no entry to the long hearts. I am about to do this when another thought occurs. Leading a *low* trump lets us keep everything under
control. I am bound to regain the lead however declarer plays. When
this happens, I can make sure dummy's last trump is drawn and then
knock out the ♠A. This is surely the safest option.

Declarer wins my trump switch in hand with the jack and
returns the suit. I win with the ace, perforce, and then lead a spade.
The ace goes up and, when South drops the nine, it becomes clear
why a spade at Trick 2 would not have worked. Declarer would
have ducked in dummy, letting partner win the trick. Later a ruffing spade finesse would have set up a second spade winner in
dummy, enabling declarer to make two discards.

Returning to the actual sequence, declarer leads the ♠2 off
dummy and partner plays low. Declarer ruffs and draws the last
trump, on which I need to find a discard.

```
                  ♠ J 10
                  ♡ K 8 6 5 2
                  ◊ 7
                  ♣ —
  ♠ 7 3                    ┌─────────┐
  ♡ Q 10 7                 │    N    │
  ◊ K J 9            W     │ W     E │    E
  ♣ —                      │    S    │
                           └─────────┘
```

If I let go a spade, declarer might lead another trump, when I shall
have to throw a major-suit card. Then declarer can cash the ♡A-K,
remove my last exit card via a ruff and, if he has ◊Q-10-x, endplay
me. True, he may prefer to finesse East for the ◊J, but can you suggest any reason why I should take the chance? I discard a heart.

When declarer plays another trump, I discard another heart and partner the ◇6. Then he cashes the ace-king of hearts and I discard the ◇9. Finally, he tries a diamond to the ten. I win with the jack and exit with a spade to put the contract one down, the full deal being:

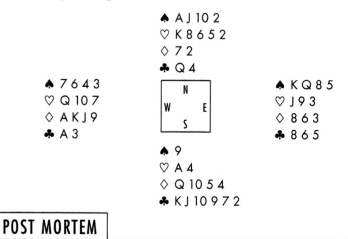

```
                    ♠ A J 10 2
                    ♡ K 8 6 5 2
                    ◇ 7 2
                    ♣ Q 4
    ♠ 7 6 4 3          N           ♠ K Q 8 5
    ♡ Q 10 7     W         E       ♡ J 9 3
    ◇ A K J 9                      ◇ 8 6 3
    ♣ A 3              S           ♣ 8 6 5
                    ♠ 9
                    ♡ A 4
                    ◇ Q 10 5 4
                    ♣ K J 10 9 7 2
```

POST MORTEM

Leading away from the ace of trumps is a tactic worth noting. The trump ace is a vital control card and you should not lightly part with it. One can even construct hands requiring a more spectacular underlead:

```
                    ♠ 7 5
                    ♡ 8 6 4
                    ◇ K J 7 4
                    ♣ Q J 10 6
    ♠ A K 10 8 2       N           ♠ Q J 3
    ♡ A K 3      W         E       ♡ 7 5
    ◇ 6 2                          ◇ Q 10 8 5 3
    ♣ 8 5 2           S           ♣ 9 7 4
                    ♠ 9 6 4
                    ♡ Q J 10 9 2
                    ◇ A 9
                    ♣ A K 3
```

South plays in 3♡. West leads a top spade and East drops the queen, showing ♠Q-J. The only way to beat the contract is for West to switch to the ♡3! If declarer returns a major, West can cash out. If not, East can deal with any attempt to take four rounds of clubs or a diamond finesse.

Many average players believe that expert defenders spend their lives making flamboyant plays: ruffing partner's winners or the underlead in the last Post Mortem, for instance. Although it is true that journalists will tend to report extraordinary plays, it is because they make good copy. Their frequency is often exaggerated. Most good players only do something flashy if it offers the chance to defeat the contract. They value winning and partnership trust too highly to do otherwise. That said, they naturally have a better awareness than most of when the 'normal' play will fail.

'This is your hand,' my friend David says in an e-mail:

♠ 3   ♡ 8 5 4 3   ◇ K Q 2   ♣ Q 10 8 3 2

'In the final of an important congress, you are fourth in hand with both sides vulnerable. You play weak jump overcalls and the bidding proceeds as follows:

WEST	NORTH	EAST	SOUTH
	1◇	2♠	3NT
all pass			

You obediently lead the ♠3 and this is what you see:

```
              ♠ 9 7 5
              ♡ K Q 7
              ◇ A 10 9 8 5
              ♣ K 4
  ♠ 3        ┌─────────┐
  ♡ 8 5 4 3  │    N    │
  ◇ K Q 2    │ W     E │
  ♣ Q 10 8 3 2│   S    │
              └─────────┘
```

I reply: 'The lead was a close decision. With my values and singleton spade, it sounds unlikely that we can set up the spades. As against that, a spade can hardly give anything away.'

'Julian, I have good news for you. Partner wins the first two tricks with the ♠K and ♠A, South playing the ten and jack. What do you discard?'

'Prospects do not seem too bright. South, to jump to 3NT, must have about 13 points. That leaves partner with only about a jack more. Most likely, declarer's hand looks like one of these:

♠ Q J 10	♠ Q J 10	♠ Q J 10
♡ A J 10	♡ A J 10	♡ A J 10
◊ J 6 3	◊ 7 6 4 3	◊ 7 6 3
♣ A 9 7 5	♣ A J 7	♣ A J 9 7

There is nothing we can do about the first hand. If we play three rounds of spades, declarer can afford the safety play in diamonds, cashing the ace in case partner has a singleton king or queen. We might score two spades and two diamonds but nothing else. We fare even worse if partner shifts to a club. Declarer can play the diamonds normally, finessing against me, and we concede an over-trick.

Our position is not so different against the second hand. If we play three rounds of spades, declarer loses two diamonds to me, this time without the option of playing the suit for one loser. If, instead, partner switches to a club, declarer simply has to play low from hand, conserving the A-J of clubs as a tenace, to stop us from scoring any club tricks. It would help, of course if partner held a fourth club. Unfortunately, South's failure to make a negative double, a likely action with a 3-4-4-2 shape, along with partner's jump to 2♠, make it likely South is 3-3 in the majors, which all but rules that out.

It looks like I have to play declarer for the third hand. Now that partner has ◊J-x there is a way to create an entry to the long spades. I discard the king of diamonds now and, if partner plays a third round of spades, the queen of diamonds. Declarer has only seven top tricks, one spade, three hearts, one diamond and two clubs and will have to try to set up the diamonds. I can afford to be endplayed once in clubs.'

'You've got it. If you don't discard your ◊K-Q, declarer executes a simple avoidance play in the suit, leading low from hand and ducking if the king or queen appears. This was the full deal:

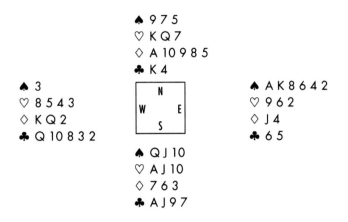

```
            ♠ 9 7 5
            ♡ K Q 7
            ◇ A 10 9 8 5
            ♣ K 4
♠ 3                              ♠ A K 8 6 4 2
♡ 8 5 4 3          N             ♡ 9 6 2
◇ K Q 2        W       E         ◇ J 4
♣ Q 10 8 3 2       S             ♣ 6 5
            ♠ Q J 10
            ♡ A J 10
            ◇ 7 6 3
            ♣ A J 9 7
```

POST MORTEM

Although opportunities to discard two high cards occur very rarely, it is reasonably common to discard one. Here are a few suits that declarer wants to establish without allowing East on lead:

$$◇ \text{ A K 9 8 5}$$

$$◇ \text{ Q 10 2} \qquad \square \qquad ◇ \text{ J 6 4}$$

$$◇ \text{ 7 3}$$

Declarer's plan is to lead twice towards the ace-king, ducking if the queen appears. Discarding the queen would thwart this plan.

$$◇ \text{ A J 9 8 5}$$

$$◇ \text{ K 2} \qquad \square \qquad ◇ \text{ Q 4}$$

$$◇ \text{ 10 7 6 3}$$

Now declarer needs to lead only once towards dummy, this time with the intention of playing the ace on a low card or ducking the king. If West can get rid of the king on another suit, this plan fails.

$\diamond$ K 8 5

$\diamond$ A 10 ☐ $\diamond$ Q 4

$\diamond$ J 9 7 6 4 3

Yet again, the defenders can score just the one trick in the suit, assuming declarer has no entry problems. For East to be the one to score it, West needs somehow to dispose of the ace.

If you are aware of these possibilities, you may be ready next time you need to make an entry-creating discard!

Choice of Poisons

The principle that jump raises of an overcall are preemptive has been around for a while. Advancer needs to make a cuebid of opener's suit to show a raise based on high-card values. In recent years it has become almost as common to play preemptive jump raises in response to an opening bid when an opponent overcalls, again with a cuebid used to show a raise based on high-card values. The law of total tricks, as expounded by Larry Cohen in *To Bid Or Not To Bid*, has no doubt played a part in this.

In a duplicate club with only the opponents vulnerable I pick up:

♠ A K Q 10 4   ♡ 8 6   ◇ J 9 4   ♣ A 7 6

The charming lady on my right opens 1♡ and I overcall 1♠. The player on my left bids 2♠ and my partner passes. After opener attempts to sign off in 3♡, her partner puts her to game to complete the auction:

WEST	NORTH	EAST	SOUTH
		pass	1♡
1♠	2♠	pass	3♡
pass	4♡	all pass	

Following the obvious ♠A lead, dummy comes down with this:

```
              ♠ 6 2
              ♡ A 10 3
              ◇ K 7 5
              ♣ K Q 10 9 3
♠ A K Q 10 4    ┌─────────┐
♡ 8 6           │    N    │
◇ J 9 4         │ W     E │
♣ A 7 6         │    S    │
                └─────────┘
```

My partner, Lawrence, plays the ♠3, which I take as a discouraging card. What do you think is the best way to continue?

Firstly, I dismiss a trump switch. To ruff a spade in dummy, declarer needs to lose the lead only once, so I can never draw dummy's trumps. Besides, there is a long club suit on which to discard her losers.

Secondly, I rule out continuing spades. Partner would not normally play low from a doubleton and, if this time he has, it means he cannot overruff the ♡10. Assuming that South would open 1♠ with 5-5 in the majors, partner is most unlikely to hold a singleton spade either.

Thirdly, I consider the diamonds. Again, time seems to be against us. East may have the ◊Q but, with just one club stopper, we will not have the chance to set up and cash a diamond trick. On the bidding, he cannot have the ◊A because that leaves South with at best a poor 10 points.

Do you think a club switch might work? Playing ace and another will beat the contract by two tricks if East started with a singleton club. Alas, this seems unlikely. With four spades and a singleton, he would surely have raised to suggest a sacrifice, and he can only have one club without four spades if South is 3-5-1-4 with the ◊A singleton. Taking a slight risk, I switch to the ♣6.

Declarer wins in dummy with the king, partner playing the eight, and draws two rounds of trumps with the king and ace, partner playing the seven and four. She abandons trumps at this point, leading the ♣J. I win with the ace and partner plays the two. Having seen a high-low from him in two suits, it is clear what to do next. (The one in clubs implies an even number of clubs, a doubleton no doubt, whilst his trump echo indicates a third trump and a desire to ruff.) Cash the ♠Q and give partner a club ruff. This was the full deal:

```
                ♠ 6 2
                ♡ A 10 3
                ◊ K 7 5
                ♣ K Q 10 9 3
  ♠ A K Q 10 4    ┌─────────┐    ♠ 8 7 3
  ♡ 8 6           │    N    │    ♡ 9 7 4
  ◊ J 9 4       W │         │ E  ◊ Q 10 8 6 3
  ♣ A 7 6         │    S    │    ♣ 8 2
                └─────────┘
                ♠ J 9 5
                ♡ K Q J 5 2
                ◊ A 2
                ♣ J 5 4
```

'Does it help if you draw a third round of trumps?' North inquiries. 'No, in that case the contract always goes down,' South replies. 'I would have three spades and a club to lose off the top. At least the way I played it, there was the chance that the defender short in clubs was also short in trumps or that West could never put his partner in to give him a ruff.'

You may have spotted that, if declarer had a singleton club, my switch could have cost an overtrick. I judged that this was unlikely given her failure to bid game over 2♠ or even to make a trial bid of 3◊. I also knew it could be vital to beat the contract if she had opened on 11 points (give East any of her jacks). Then a fair proportion of the field would not open and so probably would not reach game. At matchpoint pairs, any game that is bid and made against you that is not totally obvious usually gives you an average minus. This makes it worth taking the slight risk of conceding an overtrick to beat it.

Many players readily spot the potential for a ruff in their own hands. It is a smaller group who are equally adept at foreseeing the possibility of giving their partners a ruff. A lead of a low card from ace to three or ace to four will often produce a ruff if partner holds K-x in the suit or a low doubleton and a trump entry. A lead away from the king can also prove effective on many layouts, sometimes even in a suit declarer has bid:

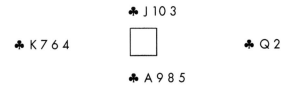

♣ J 10 3

♣ K 7 6 4   ♣ Q 2

♣ A 9 8 5

A low club to the queen may place declarer in an unpleasant dilemma: take the ace and risk losing a ruff if either defender gains the lead before trumps are drawn, or duck and risk losing to the king as well.

The benefit of leading away from the king is even more apparent on this layout:

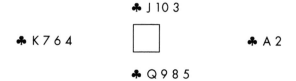

♣ J 10 3

♣ K 7 6 4   ♣ A 2

♣ Q 9 8 5

On both layouts, West's poor club spots make a slow club trick unlikely. This is a factor in deciding to play for a ruff. Of course, you also need to consider whether dummy has a long suit on which declarer can take discards: your king might run away if you lead into the ace-queen.

For decades, a debate has raged about whether you should play count or attitude signals on partner's lead. One side argues that it is easier to work out the layout of the high cards than the distribution, which makes a count signal more useful. The other says that it is more critical to know whether partner likes the suit than it is to have an exact count, making an attitude signal the more helpful. In recent years, a meeting of minds has come about, playing the primary signal as attitude with a change to count if the dummy or bidding or lead makes it unlikely that attitude will help. Another compromise is to play attitude on an ace or queen lead and otherwise count. My partner, John, and I had agreed this last when I pick up:

♠ 4 2   ♡ A J 8 5   ◇ Q 10 8 4   ♣ A K J

The bidding is as shown below, with North's 2NT (when followed by a pass over 3♠) equivalent to a limit raise in an uncontested auction:

WEST	NORTH	EAST	SOUTH
			1♠
dbl	2NT	pass	3♠
all pass			

Wanting to find out who has the ♣Q, I, as West, lead the ♣A and see:

♠ A 10 9 7
♡ 9 7 4
◇ A K 6
♣ 7 4 3

♠ 4 2
♡ A J 8 5
◇ Q 10 8 4
♣ A K J

$$\begin{array}{c} N \\ W \quad\quad E \\ S \end{array}$$

'Sorry if it's too much,' North remarks. 'My hand has some good controls.'

'I'll try not to make any overtricks,' South says, grinning.

Partner follows with the ♣2, a discouraging card which surely also denies the queen. This makes it right to switch. Since South figures to holds the ♡K and may hold the ◊J as well, I lead a trump next.

Declarer wins the trump cheaply in hand and leads the ◊J. After I cover with the ◊Q, dummy plays the ace, king and another diamond. John follows with the five, the three and the two, whilst South, having played the ◊7 on the second round, ruffs the third. John, who clearly began with ◊9-5-3-2, has played them to indicate neutral preference between clubs and hearts. Next comes a trump to dummy's ace and I find that partner began with J-x. These cards are left as the ♡4 is led to the two and king:

```
              ♠ 10 9
              ♡ 9 7 4
              ◊ —
              ♣ 7 4
  ♠ —              ┌─────────┐
  ♡ A J 8 5        │    N    │
  ◊ 8              │ W     E │
  ♣ K J            │    S    │
                   └─────────┘
```

In some circumstances, it can work well to duck with A-J, if I think the hand on my right has K-Q-10. The effect is to leave my opponent on lead so I can score the ace and jack later, rather than risk endplaying myself. Can you see why this would not work here? It will do me no good to make two heart tricks if I then have to concede a ruff and discard or set up South's ♣Q. Even giving partner the ♡10, trouble looms if I win with the ace and return a low heart. Dummy's seven (or nine) will force out his ten and again I shall find myself on play after winning the third round of hearts. Nor will it help to hope that partner has played the ♡2 from 10-2 doubleton rather than a three-card holding. In this case, declarer will have a 5-4-2-2 shape and we can only ever score two hearts and two clubs. In extremis, I could play John for ♡Q-2 doubleton, although that would make South's play of the ♡K (as opposed to the ♡10) completely daft.

Since the idea is to win two heart tricks, partner winning the second, I take the ♡A and return the jack. After declarer wins with the queen and exits with a third round, John wins and leads a club. I make both the king and jack to set the contract, the full deal being as follows:

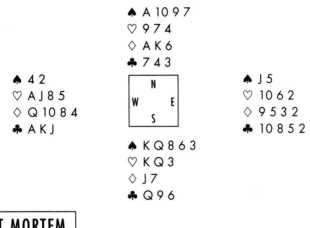

```
                    ♠ A 10 9 7
                    ♡ 9 7 4
                    ◊ A K 6
                    ♣ 7 4 3
     ♠ 4 2              N          ♠ J 5
     ♡ A J 8 5       W     E       ♡ 10 6 2
     ◊ Q 10 8 4        S           ◊ 9 5 3 2
     ♣ A K J                       ♣ 10 8 5 2
                    ♠ K Q 8 6 3
                    ♡ K Q 3
                    ◊ J 7
                    ♣ Q 9 6
```

POST MORTEM

North-South did well to stay out of game with 24 points and a nine-card fit. South correctly took a dim view of having no aces, whilst North knew that a 4333 shape generates few tricks and that finesses were likely to fail given my double. In a pairs event, -140 for us would score very badly.

This was the position after the ♣A, two rounds of trumps and three rounds of diamonds:

```
                    ♠ 10 9
                    ♡ 9 7 4
                    ◊ —
                    ♣ 7 4
     ♠ —               N          ♠ —
     ♡ A J 8 5       W     E       ♡ 10 6 2
     ◊ 8               S           ◊ 9
     ♣ K J                         ♣ 10 8 5
                    ♠ K Q
                    ♡ K Q 3
                    ◊ —
                    ♣ Q 9
```

When a heart to the king lost to the ace, there was still a chance I had A-J-10-x or any five hearts and would be left on play.

Finally, note that we should still have beaten the contract playing count signals. A trump switch at Trick 2 would still be right, but now John must play his diamonds as suit preference, say the ◊9 on the second round.

As dealer with both sides vulnerable, I pick up the following hand in a pairs event at my long-time local club, Basingstoke:

♠ K 2   ♡ A K 10 6 5 2   ◊ 10 6 5 3   ♣ 5

Vulnerable, certainly, a weak two (or Multi) can have 10 points. Still, this hand is too good. I apply the HLQT (or Hi-Li-Cute) method, which Ron Klinger designed and is fast becoming *the* yardstick for judging whether a hand warrants a one-level opening. You count 10 points in high cards, ten cards in the longest two suits and two and a half quick tricks (defensive tricks). This totals 22.5, with 22 needed for a sound vulnerable opening.

As it happens, it soon becomes apparent that it would probably have made no difference if I had opened a heavy 'Trent/Granovetter style' 2♡. North makes a simple overcall in diamonds and South jumps all the way to 6♣, giving us this quick auction to a slam:

WEST	NORTH	EAST	SOUTH
1♡	2◊	pass	6♣
all pass			

I lead the ♡K (king from ace-king against slams) and this is what we see:

```
              ♠ J 7
              ♡ Q 9 3
              ◊ A K Q J 7 4
              ♣ 9 7
♠ K 2              ┌─────────┐
♡ A K 10 6 5 2     │    N    │
◊ 10 6 5 3         │ W     E │
♣ 5                │    S    │
                   └─────────┘
```

My partner, Sheena, plays the ♡4 (standard count) and South the ♡8.

South would hardly have jumped to 6♠ with J-8-4 in the suit likely to be led and the chance of scoring two heart tricks seems remote indeed. In this case, prospects overall do not look too good. South surely has the ♠A and running clubs, and dummy contains all those diamond winners. We cannot do anything about a massive club suit or the ♠A but perhaps there is a way to kill the diamonds. Here are a few potential hands for declarer that spring to mind:

♠ A Q 6	♠ A Q 9 6	♠ A Q 9 6
♡ 8	♡ 8	♡ 8
◇ 8	◇ 8	◇ —
♣ A K Q 10 6 4 3 2	♣ A K Q 10 6 4 3	♣ A K Q 10 8 4 3 2

Against the first hand, the best I can do is to play a diamond. Declarer has three options now: (i) cash the ♣A in the hope the jack falls so that the ♣9 will be a re-entry to the long diamonds, (ii) finesse Sheena for the ♠K, which is impossible on the bidding, or (iii) play on diamonds, hoping either for a 3-3 break or that East is short. The third option is by far the most attractive and it will work. After overruffing Sheena on the third round of diamonds, declarer can draw our remaining trumps in one round and cross to the ♣9 to continue playing diamonds.

The diamond switch would prove effective against the second hand. Alas, the bidding indicates otherwise. Players at our club very rarely bid a slam without checking on aces. With this hand, South would surely have bid 4NT over 2◇, planning to pass a 5♣ (no aces) response or convert 5◇ to 6♣. If our opponents were playing Roman Keycard, the inference would be less strong: South might worry that North would count the ◇K as an ace. I know, however, that my present opponents play simple Blackwood.

The third hand sounds right — South's failure to go via 4NT hints at a void somewhere. Unfortunately, a diamond shift now will let declarer take three fast diamond tricks — enough for the contract. If partner has three diamonds and two clubs higher than the seven, a trump switch would work but, if South's clubs are as good as shown, a trump will concede an entry to dummy. A spade switch clearly will not work either. Even if declarer forgets to put up dummy's jack, a spade ruff will create an entry to dummy. By a process of elimination, leading a second heart has to be right. It goes against the grain to set up dummy's queen, but what use is one more winner in an entryless dummy? I put the ♡A on the table.

Having ruffed the second heart, declarer lays down the ♣A and looks worried when I play the five and Sheena the six. An avalanche of trumps follows but it becomes increasingly obvious that the ♠K is going to score and we beat the slam by a trick. This was the full deal:

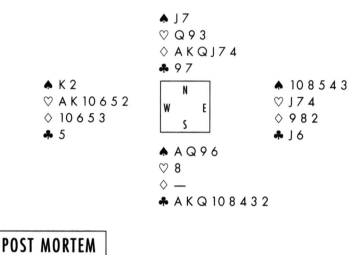

```
                        ♠ J 7
                        ♡ Q 9 3
                        ◇ A K Q J 7 4
                        ♣ 9 7
   ♠ K 2                  ┌─────────┐        ♠ 10 8 5 4 3
   ♡ A K 10 6 5 2         │    N    │        ♡ J 7 4
   ◇ 10 6 5 3           W │       E │        ◇ 9 8 2
   ♣ 5                    │    S    │        ♣ J 6
                          └─────────┘
                        ♠ A Q 9 6
                        ♡ 8
                        ◇ —
                        ♣ A K Q 10 8 4 3 2
```

POST MORTEM

Identifying an entryless dummy so early in the play is rare. Setting up a winner there by leading a card that you expect declarer to ruff happens more often in a position like this:

```
                        ♠ K Q 9 4
                        ♡ Q J 6
                        ◇ K 8 3
                        ♣ K 10 5
   ♠ A                    ┌─────────┐        ♠ 5 2
   ♡ A K 9 8 5 3 2        │    N    │        ♡ 10 4
   ◇ J 10               W │       E │        ◇ Q 7 6 5 2
   ♣ Q 7 2                │    S    │        ♣ J 9 6 3
                          └─────────┘
                        ♠ J 10 8 7 6 3
                        ♡ 7
                        ◇ A 9 4
                        ♣ A 8 4
```

As West, having cashed a top heart against 4♠, you can continue with a second round. Unless South has a seven-card spade suit, you can play a third round after you come in with the ♠A to let partner ruff and prevent a discard. This is the only way to beat the contract as the cards lie.

Being human, we all react to certain events at the table. Suppose you lead the king (from K-Q-10) and dummy puts down J-x-x. Your heart sinks. It lifts, though, when your king holds. Now imagine you lead your long suit against 3NT and knock out declarer's sole stopper in the suit. Your initial feeling of happiness can easily turn to depression if declarer rattles off a load of winners in other suits. The important thing is not to allow this roller coaster of emotions to deflect you from the three most vital defensive tasks: counting, counting and counting (in no particular order), points, tricks and distribution.

♠ 5 ♡ J 10 5 4 3 ◇ A 10 9 8 4 ♣ A J

With the other side vulnerable, I would expect to bid on this hand. In the event, I observe this sequence, with 2NT 20-22, and 3♣ simple Stayman:

WEST	NORTH	EAST	SOUTH
	pass	pass	2NT
pass	3♣	pass	3♡
pass	3NT	all pass	

Even without knowing that South holds four hearts, I would probably lead the ◇10. Now the choice is clear-cut. This dummy appears:

```
              ♠ A Q J 9
              ♡ 8 6 2
              ◇ J
              ♣ 8 7 6 5 4
♠ 5               N
♡ J 10 5 4 3   W     E
◇ A 10 9 8 4      S
♣ A J
```

Although the 8 points in dummy come as a disappointment, prospects brighten when partner covers the ◇J with the queen and drives out the king. Declarer lays down the ♠K, partner playing the two (standard count), and continues with a spade to the ace. I discard the ♡3 on this and can spare the ♣J on the third round of spades. On the fourth round of spades, South discards a diamond. What do you suggest I should do?

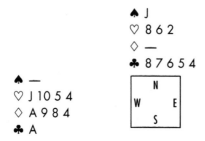

```
              ♠ J
              ♡ 8 6 2
              ◊ —
              ♣ 8 7 6 5 4
♠ —              ┌─────────┐
♡ J 10 5 4       │    N    │
◊ A 9 8 4      W │         │ E
♣ A              │    S    │
                 └─────────┘
```

Maybe the time has come to take my own advice and do some counting. South has shown at least 20 points and there were 18 between
my hand and dummy. This means the ◊Q was partner's only honor
card. Armed with this information, it is possible to count declarer's
tricks: four spades, three hearts (A-K-Q) and a diamond.

Apart from the spade suit, the distribution seems less certain.
Even so, do you agree that there seems to be enough information for
me to decide what to do on this trick? South, who bid 3♡, has not
discarded one, so must have four hearts left. Letting a heart go
would thus be fatal. Since throwing the ♣A would bring even
greater disaster, I have to part with a diamond. The danger of
course is that declarer might test the hearts and, finding the bad
break, knock out my ♣A. If we score just three diamonds and a club
then the contract will make. I need to find a way to reach partner's
long spade and can only do that by letting go a high diamond. With
my ◊A-9-8 now sequential, I throw the ◊A.

As expected, declarer next cashes two hearts. I follow with the
four and then drop the jack. Partner follows once before discarding
the ♣2. Now comes the ♣K and my ace wins as partner follows
with the three.

There are two possible plays at this point. If East began with
◊Q-7-x, I need to lead a low diamond. If, instead, South has the ◊7,
then I need to cash the eight, lead a low one and hope partner has a
fourth one to lead back. It hits me that I have not been paying close
attention to the spades. Luckily, this is probably immaterial.
Nobody could really expect partner to give a suit-preference signal
from ◊Q-6-x-x and not ◊Q-7-x or vice versa.

Fortunately, I did spot partner's first discard, the ♣2, and the ♣3
on the first round of clubs. The two followed by the three, playing
standard count, surely shows an odd number of clubs, in this case
three. This means South began with a 3-4-3-3 shape, making it best
for me to cash a high diamond. I carry this through and know it is

the right thing to do when the seven falls on my right. I lead the ◊4 next and partner wins, cashes the long spade, on which I throw a heart, and returns a diamond. Declarer works out that I shall have to overtake and discards the ♣Q to get out for one down. The full deal is as follows:

```
                    ♠ A Q J 9
                    ♡ 8 6 2
                    ◊ J
                    ♣ 8 7 6 5 4
  ♠ 5                                    ♠ 10 7 6 3 2
  ♡ J 10 5 4 3        ┌─────────┐        ♡ 9
  ◊ A 10 9 8 4        │ N       │        ◊ Q 6 5 2
  ♣ A J             W │       E │        ♣ 10 3 2
                      │    S    │
                      └─────────┘
                    ♠ K 8 4
                    ♡ A K Q 7
                    ◊ K 7 3
                    ♣ K Q 9
```

POST MORTEM

This was the position as the fourth round of spades was led:

```
                    ♠ J
                    ♡ 8 6 2
                    ◊ —
                    ♣ 8 7 6 5 4
  ♠ —                                    ♠ 10 7
  ♡ J 10 5 4          ┌─────────┐        ♡ 9
  ◊ A 9 8 4           │ N       │        ◊ 6 5 2
  ♣ A               W │       E │        ♣ 10 3 2
                      │    S    │
                      └─────────┘
                    ♠ —
                    ♡ A K Q 7
                    ◊ 7 3
                    ♣ K Q 9
```

Even if South were to throw the ♣9 here, the defenders would still prevail so long as West does the right things with his diamonds.

Great Recovery

During the bidding and early play, bridge is a game of probabilities and percentages rather than certainties. One should choose an action that stands the best chance of working in the long run, knowing that it may not work on the precise deal you are playing. At duplicate, especially in a match, if a normal early action backfires, you can take comfort from the fact that others holding your cards may make the same choice. You can then focus on trying to outdo them from that point onwards.

Third in hand, and with only the opposing side vulnerable, I pick up this hand in a local league match:

♠ K 9 4   ♡ K Q 8   ◇ 8 5   ♣ J 10 8 7 3

Our opponents conduct an uncontested sequence to 4♡ as follows:

WEST	NORTH	EAST	SOUTH
		pass	1♡
pass	1♠	pass	2◇
pass	3♡	pass	4♡
all pass			

I naturally lead the ♣J and this shapeless dummy comes down:

```
            ♠ Q J 8 3
            ♡ 7 5 2
            ◇ K 9 3
            ♣ A Q 4
♠ K 9 4        ┌─────────┐
♡ K Q 8        │    N    │
◇ 8 5          │ W     E │
♣ J 10 8 7 3   │    S    │
               └─────────┘
```

Declarer plays low from dummy and wins in hand with the king, partner following with the two. A club comes straight back and I can guess what is coming. Partner follows with the nine on the second round of clubs and the five on the third as South discards a low spade. Now comes a heart to the four, ten and queen. What do you think I should lead to the next trick?

```
            ♠ Q J 8 3
            ♡ 7 5
            ◇ K 9 3
            ♣ —
  ♠ K 9 4      ┌─────────┐
  ♡ K 8        │    N    │
  ◇ 8 5        │ W     E │
  ♣ 8 3        │    S    │
              └─────────┘
```

Partner's ♣9 was surely a suit-preference signal for spades, showing the ace, and declarer's rush to discard a spade confirms this.
Evidently, we would have been better placed on an initial spade
lead. Sadly, turning back the clock is impossible.

Since the bidding marks South with nine cards in the red suits,
we can score at most one spade trick now. Assuming East has the
♠A, South must have the ♡A and good diamonds as well. We are
unlikely to have a third-round diamond winner — partner would
need both the queen and the jack for that — but a fourth-round winner seems a reasonable prospect. The trouble is that declarer may
intend to cash the ♡A after regaining the lead, leaving the master
trump out but keeping one in dummy for ruffing the fourth round
of diamonds if necessary. It therefore seems that if we do nothing
special we will end up with two trumps and a spade.

Suddenly I have an idea. If partner's remaining trump is the
jack, an uppercut on the fourth round of clubs will promote my ♡8.
(It is hopeless if South has the rest of the trumps because then we
will have no spade trick.) Clearly, it will do no good to play the
fourth club yet. Rather than overruffing with the ♡A, declarer will
discard a losing spade. Standard defensive technique is to cash
one's side winners before trying for a trump promotion and, with
the need to retain the lead clear, I lay down the ♠K. This holds and
I duly lead a club. A low diamond goes from dummy and partner
produces the hoped-for ♡J, South overruffing with the ♡A.

When declarer crosses to the ◇K and leads a trump, I take my
two winners and partner ends up with the last trick for down two.
This is the full deal:

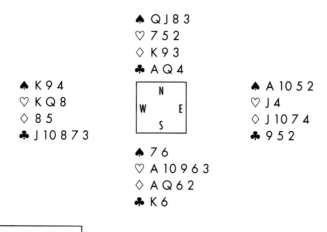

'Sorry, I can get out for one down by leaving both trumps out at the end,' South remarks. 'I was hoping that either the last two trumps would fall together or, if East had both, that the diamonds would divide evenly.'

'Does it help if you play ace and other trump instead of leading to the ten?' North asks. 'You avoid the promotion if you do that.'

'It makes no difference,' South replies, with a glance in my direction. 'West can draw two rounds of trumps, on which East discards a spade. Then, unless West plays the ♠K on the first round of spades to expose his partner to a squeeze, I have a diamond loser. You wouldn't have done that, would you?' I nod my head affirmatively.

North says, 'I thought about rebidding 2NT because my hand had no ruffing value and my black queens would not be pulling full weight in a heart contract. Can we make 3NT?'

'It goes down on a spade lead to the king and a spade back if East ducks your queen,' South replies. 'The defenders score three spades and two hearts. Now, while I guess that East is more likely to start with a club, since you have two heart stoppers to knock out, the defenders have time to switch to spades. To beat 3NT, it looks as though West must switch to a low spade and East needs to let your queen win. Whether they find this may depend a bit on how clear it is that you have ♣A-Q-x. 3NT is a better contract because it stands a very good chance if diamonds break 3-3. Perhaps I could have bid it myself, but ♣K-x seemed a bit of a shaky stopper.'

People sometimes ask how I cope with playing different conventions or systems with different partners. The truth is that it is usually little trouble. For example, on sitting down with Graham, I think intermediate twos, reverse count and even/odd discards (we used to call them odd/even until we found that we are unusual in playing even cards as encouraging). Changing something with a partner is harder. I might remember talking about a possible change but not whether we agreed on it.

Playing with Graham in a match, with both sides vulnerable, I pick up:

♠ Q 10 8 2   ♡ K 8   ◇ A K Q 6   ♣ J 9 6

South opens 1♠ and I overcall 1NT. North doubles and Graham bids 2◇ (a transfer with him despite the double). Eventually South reaches 4♠:

WEST	NORTH	EAST	SOUTH
			1♠
1NT	dbl	2◇	pass
2♡	3♠	pass	4♠
all pass			

I lead the ◇A and dummy puts down a twelve-count:

```
              ♠ J 6 5
              ♡ Q J 4
              ◇ J 5
              ♣ A K 10 5 2
♠ Q 10 8 2        ┌─────────┐
♡ K 8             │    N    │
◇ A K Q 6         │ W     E │
♣ J 9 6           │    S    │
                  └─────────┘
```

Graham follows with the ◇2 (reverse count) and I win the trick as South follows with the nine.

Do you agree that on the bidding partner's even number of diamonds is probably four? If he has a doubleton, declarer holds quite a shapely hand. We can also, with a fair degree of confidence, place the ace and king of spades and the ♡A on the right. Without these cards, South would hardly have an opening bid, let alone enough to advance to 4♠.

Dummy is now down to a singleton diamond and, knowing that I cannot prevent a single ruff, I decide to continue with the ◇Q. Perhaps partner will follow with his lowest diamond, suggesting that he holds the ♣Q. No, he plays the seven. I can almost write down everyone's hand now. The one thing still in doubt is whether South's shape is 5-3-3-2, 5-2-3-3 or, less likely, 6-2-3-2.

If declarer has a doubleton club, leading a club now and a second one when I come in with the ♠Q will sever communications with dummy, meaning my ♡K scores at the end. However, this will not work if East is the one with two clubs. Then dummy will have an easy club entry.

I decide to continue with a third round of diamonds. Since declarer will have to play a club to the queen anyway to start trumps from hand, we are no worse off than if I played a club myself, and this will block the trumps. As expected, declarer ruffs the third diamond in dummy, plays a club to the three, queen and nine and then leads a low spade. Obviously, I go in with my ♠Q. These are the cards left on view:

$$\begin{array}{c}
\spadesuit \ J \\
\heartsuit \ Q \ J \ 4 \\
\diamondsuit \ - \\
\clubsuit \ A \ K \ 10 \ 5
\end{array}$$

```
  ♠ 10 8 2        ┌─────────┐
  ♡ K 8           │    N    │
  ◇ 6             │ W     E │
  ♣ J 6           │    S    │
                  └─────────┘
```

A trump lead will achieve nothing. After taking the jack, declarer will come to hand with the ♡A and draw my remaining trumps. A club is equally futile. Partner's play of the three on the first round, the lowest club he could have, must show a doubleton. This means I cannot cut declarer off from dummy. Nor will a diamond get us anywhere. Declarer ruffs in hand, crosses to the ♠J, and comes back to the ♡A to draw my last trump.

You have probably noticed a recurring theme in these lines: declarer uses the ♡A as an entry to come back to hand to draw my

trumps. I can probably thwart this plan by leading the ♡K now.
When the ♡A wins this trick and the ♠J the next, the long pause
after Graham shows out tells me that the contract is going down.
Evidently, there is no way back to draw my trumps. Eventually
declarer cashes dummy's ♡Q and ruffs the ♡J. Naturally I overruff
and we have the contract down. This was the full deal:

```
              ♠ J 6 5
              ♡ Q J 4
              ◇ J 5
              ♣ A K 10 5 2
♠ Q 10 8 2    ┌─────────┐    ♠ 3
♡ K 8         │    N    │    ♡ 10 9 6 5 3 2
◇ A K Q 6     │ W     E │    ◇ 8 7 3 2
♣ J 9 6       │    S    │    ♣ 8 3
              └─────────┘
              ♠ A K 9 7 4
              ♡ A 7
              ◇ 10 9 4
              ♣ Q 7 4
```

POST MORTEM

This was the position after three rounds of diamonds, a club to the
queen and a spade to West's queen:

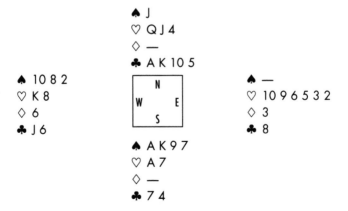

```
              ♠ J
              ♡ Q J 4
              ◇ —
              ♣ A K 10 5
♠ 10 8 2      ┌─────────┐    ♠ —
♡ K 8         │    N    │    ♡ 10 9 6 5 3 2
◇ 6           │ W     E │    ◇ 3
♣ J 6         │    S    │    ♣ 8
              └─────────┘
              ♠ A K 9 7
              ♡ A 7
              ◇ —
              ♣ 7 4
```

After West exits with the ♡K, declarer cannot avoid a trump promotion.

Odds-on Bet

40

The Spring Foursomes is the premier tournament event in the UK. It attracts a number of international entrants and very few weak teams take part. It involves playing up to seven thirty-two board matches over four days. The competition's brochure describes the event as 'not for the faint-hearted', and it certainly helps to have a team of six. This event is probably the closest equivalent to the Vanderbilt and Spingold that you might find in Europe.

In an early match with neither side vulnerable, I am dealer and hold:

♠ A K Q 3 2　♡ K 7 2　♢ A 10 2　♣ J 10

I open 1♠ and North doubles. My partner passes and South jumps to 3♣. I could double for takeout, but it sounds as if partner holds little. I pass and North bids 3♠, asking for a stopper. South's 4♣ ends the bidding:

WEST	NORTH	EAST	SOUTH
1♠	dbl	pass	3♣
pass	3♠	pass	4♣
all pass			

I lead the ♠A and dummy puts down this collection:

♠ 10 9 7
♡ Q J 10 5
♢ K Q J 9
♣ A Q

♠ A K Q 3 2	
♡ K 7 2	N
♢ A 10 2	W　　E
♣ J 10	S

My partner, Lawrence, follows with the four (standard signals) and South with the five. How do you suggest I continue?

There are 32 points between my hand and dummy, whilst South surely has the ♣K and the ♡A for the jump to 3♣. If partner's ♠4 is a singleton, we should defeat the contract if I keep playing spades.

To have no loser in a red suit, declarer needs a void in diamonds and a singleton ♡A. Of course, given South's length in clubs and reluctance to bid 3NT, it seems far more likely that East began with three spades rather than one.

Since the bidding makes it impossible for South to have five diamonds, a diamond ruff cannot provide the setting trick. Could partner have a trump trick? That would leave South with at best something like this:

♠ J 5   ♡ A 9   ◇ 8 7 6 4   ♣ K 8 7 6 5

Although some people would bid 3♣ in response to the double with that hand, do you agree it would be a minority choice? Assuming South has at least six clubs, I need to score the ♡K. Unfortunately, there is a real danger that any heart losers will disappear on dummy's diamonds.

To prevent this from happening, I can underlead my spades for a heart switch. In order to work, this needs partner to have the ♠J and South not to have a diamond void or a singleton heart. Assuming South would not bid differently with J-x or x-x of spades, there is a three in five chance that partner has the jack. This strikes me as a better bet than hoping for him to have a trump trick. I lead the ♠3 to partner's ♠J, and a heart comes back. Declarer plays low on this and my king wins. I lay down the ◇A, a necessary precaution as it turns out, because the full deal is as follows:

```
              ♠ 10 9 7
              ♡ Q J 10 5
              ◇ K Q J 9
              ♣ A Q
♠ A K Q 3 2        N        ♠ J 6 4
♡ K 7 2      W         E    ♡ 8 6 4
◇ A 10 2          S        ◇ 8 7 6 5 3
♣ J 10                     ♣ 7 4
              ♠ 8 5
              ♡ A 9 3
              ◇ 4
              ♣ K 9 8 6 5 3 2
```

As a defender with the bulk of your side's values, a problem you face time and time again is how to get partner on lead to attack a suit that you cannot play yourself. On this deal, it became apparent that East began with three spades to South's two. Clearly there was a 60% chance that the player who was dealt the three spades would hold the ♠J.

Here are some more layouts on which you might cash a top card on the first round and lead low on the second:

♠ 10 9 7

♠ A K 8 6 3   ♠ Q J 2

♠ 5 4

This is a standard situation. If East drops the queen, this guarantees the jack as well (unless it is a singleton). Provided East has a spare trump with which to ruff, West can safely continue with a low spade. Naturally, the size of West's second spade would indicate suit-preference.

♠ 10 9 7

♠ A K 8 6 3 2   ♠ Q 4

♠ J 5

When East plays the four, the lowest spade out from West's viewpoint, South can do nothing to confuse the situation. East would not play the four from either 5-4 or J-4. This makes only two holdings possible: a singleton four and Q-4 doubleton. As just discussed, East must not play the queen from Q-4. That play normally promises the jack and might well encourage West (now wrongly) to continue with a low card.

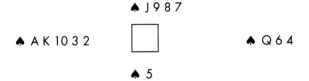

♠ J 9 8 7

♠ A K 10 3 2   ♠ Q 6 4

♠ 5

This position is similar. Since East's play of the four cannot be from 6-4 or 5-4, it must be from Q-4, a singleton four or (if count) Q-x-4. Assuming this is a side suit in a contract, East cannot actually gain the lead on the second round. Still, it may help for West to continue with a low card. Declarer will have no way to set up dummy's jack by ruffing and, if East gains the lead in some other suit, it will be safe to return a spade.

Strategic Decision

41

One special feature of the Spring Foursomes is that no team goes out of the main event until it has lost twice. This means that if you run into a team in top form early on you still have a chance. In a second-round match, I am in fourth seat and our side alone is vulnerable when I pick up:

♠ A Q 8 7 3   ♡ Q   ◇ 10 6 3   ♣ Q 10 7 4

After North opens 1♡, partner overcalls 1♠ and South bids 2◇. My choices now are a simple 4♠ or a 4♡ splinter. I opt for the former because (a) the hand contains little outside spades and (b) my ♡Q may cause partner to misjudge the value of ♡J-x-x. South reopens with 4NT, suggesting two places to play, and North bids 5◇. It sounds likely that we have ten spades and they nine diamonds, which means it may well be the case that neither 5◇ nor 5♠ will make. Since a sacrifice at this vulnerability is unlikely to prove cheap, we sell out to 5◇. The bidding has been:

WEST	NORTH	EAST	SOUTH
	1♡	1♠	2◇
4♠	pass	pass	4NT
pass	5◇	all pass	

I lead the ♠A and this collection comes down in dummy:

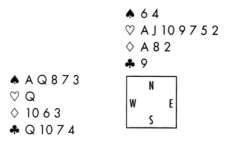

♠ 6 4
♡ A J 10 9 7 5 2
◇ A 8 2
♣ 9

♠ A Q 8 7 3
♡ Q
◇ 10 6 3
♣ Q 10 7 4

Some would have opened 4♡ on the North cards but, in my opinion, to preempt with two aces and few fillers is misleading.

My ♠A holds, as my partner, Lawrence, plays the two and South the five. Knowing that partner does not have solid opening values and that he must have a five-card suit to overcall without them, one spade trick is our limit. From where can we find two more?

It is difficult to say as yet. Here are some possible South hands:

♠ 5	♠ 5	♠ 5
♡ K 3	♡ 8	♡ 8 3
◇ Q J 9 7 5	◇ K Q 9 7 5 4	◇ K Q J 9 7 5
♣ A J 8 6 2	♣ A 8 6 5 2	♣ A J 6 2

Against the first hand, a heart switch will do the job. Then, after partner comes in with the ◇K, he can give me a ruff.

A heart switch fares less well against the second hand. Declarer wins in dummy and takes the ruffing heart finesse. I score a trump to go with my ♠A but that is all. For this hand, it looks like a club at Trick 2 offers the best chance. If declarer plays for the ruffing heart finesse, I can ruff and force dummy with a club. Another possible line for declarer would be to ruff the second round of hearts with the ◇7. What happens after that is harder to say. It seems right to discard a spade rather than overruff. After that, except by giving up a trick to the ♡K, declarer cannot set up the hearts, and partner has no need to cover whilst I have trumps left. Do you agree?

The third hand probably seems the most realistic of the three, with South holding fillers in both minors. Again, it looks like I need to guard against the threat posed by dummy's hearts, and it will not work for me to continue spades or switch to a heart. In each case, declarer simply knocks out the ♡K, ruffs partner's heart return high and draws trumps, ending in dummy. I decide therefore to switch to the ♣4.

Partner puts up the ♣K and the ♣A wins. Declarer considers how to continue, then plays a heart to the ace and a second round to partner's king. I discard the ♠3, hoping partner might read this as a suit-preference signal for clubs because my spade holding is already clear.

Sure enough, the ♣3 comes back and South plays the jack. I cover with the queen and dummy ruffs with the ◇2. Next comes a spade ruffed with the ◇5, a club ruffed with the ◇8 and a heart ruffed with the ◇9. The contract is going two down now. I overruff with the ten and return a trump. I make the last trick with the ♣10. The full deal is as follows:

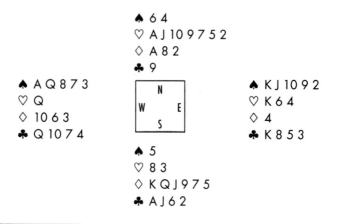

```
            ♠ 6 4
            ♡ A J 10 9 7 5 2
            ◊ A 8 2
            ♣ 9
♠ A Q 8 7 3          N           ♠ K J 10 9 2
♡ Q          W              E     ♡ K 6 4
◊ 10 6 3                          ◊ 4
♣ Q 10 7 4         S             ♣ K 8 5 3
            ♠ 5
            ♡ 8 3
            ◊ K Q J 9 7 5
            ♣ A J 6 2
```

POST MORTEM

Having spotted the need to force dummy, I had little option but to lead its shortest suit and hope that declarer could not get home on a crossruff.

Forcing the dummy can also be the solution when declarer is short of entries. Consider this layout:

```
               ♠ 3
               ♡ A 9 8 2
               ◊ J 8 7
               ♣ A Q J 8 5
♠ A J 10 8 4          N           ♠ K Q 5 2
♡ K J          W              E    ♡ 10 6 5 4 3
◊ A 6 2                           ◊ 3
♣ K 9 2             S             ♣ 7 6 3
               ♠ 9 7 6
               ♡ Q 7
               ◊ K Q 10 9 5 4
               ♣ 10 4
```

South plays in 5◊ after East-West have competed to 4♠ and West leads the ♠A. As West, there is only one sequence of plays you can make to defeat this contract. Firstly, you need to lead a second spade, which dummy ruffs. Then, when declarer plays a diamond to the king, you must take your ace at once and, finally, you lead a third round of spades. Of course, this would not work so well if South had the ♠K and East the ♡Q. Fortunately, on that layout, East would probably drop the ♠Q at Trick 1.

When to Rise

42

Barry Rigal played his Junior bridge for England, but now lives and works in the United States. We stay in touch via email, and this is from one of our exchanges.

'Hi Barry, you may recall that in our discussion about sources of material I mentioned starting with the layout of a single suit and building a full deal from it. Your *Breaking the Rules* articles in *Bridge Magazine* often provide good copy for this. Indeed, having read one of your articles, I constructed a problem with two 'second hand low, yes or no' decisions.

♠ A 7 6 5   ♡ 2   ◇ K 5   ♣ K Q 10 8 7 5

After partner passes, your right hand opponent opens one heart and, at IMP scoring with both sides vulnerable, you overcall two clubs. Before I go on, can I ask you about this bid? If we reversed the clubs and diamonds, making the shape 4-1-6-2, how would you feel about making a takeout double? I understand that quite a few US experts play a takeout double followed by converting two clubs to two diamonds as not showing extras.'

'That's true. Equal Length Conversion, as some call it, is popular in the States. It's mainstream but not majority I'd say. I do play it over a weak two myself. So if you switch the minors, then yes, double would be OK.'

'Thank you, Barry. That's nice and clear. Presumably the case for doubling would be stronger if they open one spade and you are 1-4-6-2. In that case, you cannot overcall in your long suit and hope to have a chance to bid your major at the two-level. Returning to the actual hand, over your two clubs, your left hand opponent jumps to four hearts and this becomes the final contract. Here is the auction in full:

WEST	NORTH	EAST	SOUTH
		pass	1♡
2♣	4♡	all pass	

You lead the king of clubs and this is what you see:

```
                    ♠ K 9
                    ♡ Q 10 8 6 4 3
                    ◇ A 10 6
                    ♣ J 3
    ♠ A 7 6 5      ┌─────────┐
    ♡ 2            │    N    │
    ◇ K 5          │ W     E │
    ♣ K Q 10 8 7 5 │    S    │
                   └─────────┘
```

Partner plays the ♣2 (count with the jack in dummy) and declarer's
ace wins. Declarer plays back a spade. Do you take the ace or not?
If you duck, declarer returns to hand with a trump (partner follows)
and leads a diamond. Again, Barry, do you play the king or not?'

'I think I'd duck the ♠A and consider playing the ◇K — but I'd
need to know a bit more. If declarer is 2-5-4-2 and partner has the
◇Q-J, I'd better unblock. Can we ever win two diamond tricks if
South has either the ◇Q or the ◇J? No. So I will play the ◇K.'

'Partner will play the four on the first spade and you'll be pleased
to hear that you've found the right answer. As you say, Barry, there's
no point grabbing the ♠A and cashing the ♣K to avoid being endplayed because you need partner to have the ◇Q-J anyway. Going in
with the ♠A would only be right if South is 1-5-5-2 or 1-6-4-2, but
these shapes are unlikely. In any case, if the contract is beatable, they
leave partner with ♠Q-J-x-x-x-x and ◇Q-J-x-(x), which sounds
enough for opening a weak 2♠ or perhaps bidding 4♠ over 4♡. If
South has ♠Q-x-x or ♠Q-10-x, it could prove vital to duck the spade.'

This was the full deal:

```
                    ♠ K 9
                    ♡ Q 10 8 6 4 3
                    ◇ A 10 6
                    ♣ J 3
    ♠ A 7 6 5      ┌─────────┐      ♠ J 10 4 3
    ♡ 2            │    N    │      ♡ 7
    ◇ K 5          │ W     E │      ◇ Q J 8 3 2
    ♣ K Q 10 8 7 5 │    S    │      ♣ 9 4 2
                   └─────────┘
                    ♠ Q 8 2
                    ♡ A K J 9 5
                    ◇ 9 7 4
                    ♣ A 6
```

DEFEND THESE HANDS WITH ME

After the ♠K won, declarer could have conceded a spade and ruffed a spade in dummy before coming to hand with a trump and leading a diamond. That sequence would be stronger in theory — it caters for a doubleton ♠A with West — but it would make the danger of an endplay more apparent. Maybe declarer judged that East would play a higher spade than the four from a six-card suit. Once one excludes that holding, either line works if West has a doubleton diamond and wins the second round of the suit. After West cashes the ♣Q, a spade exit, whether it sets up South's queen or gives a ruff and discard, would prove costly.

As a rule, if declarer has stripped your exit cards, or is in a position to do so, and has trumps in both hands, you must constantly stay alert to the danger of being thrown in and forced to concede a ruff and discard. Declarer's genuine endplay chance on this deal was to find West with a diamond holding of K-Q, K-J or Q-J doubleton. Against many defenders, the extra chance of K-x and a failure to unblock would also come in.

	◇ A J 6 3	
◇ K 5		◇ Q 10 8 2
	◇ 9 7 4	

This layout is similar. The slight difference is that West can freely play the king on the first round even at matchpoint scoring because there are no defensive tricks available if South has Q-x-x.

	◇ K 8 6 2	
◇ A 5		◇ Q 10 9 3
	◇ J 7 4	

Now declarer's holding is weaker but it is still important for West to take the ace on the first round to avoid the danger of a throw-in.

$\Diamond$ J 8 6 2

$\Diamond$ Q 5 $\Diamond$ A 10 9 3

$\Diamond$ K 7 4

Now the first diamond lead comes from dummy and declarer plays the king; once more West may need to unblock to avoid being thrown in.

Shut Out

43

In an inter-county qualifying event, the Tollemache, we are playing one of the weaker teams and trying to put them under as much pressure as we can. In an event of a round-robin nature, it counts for almost as much to get big scores against the weak teams as it does to hold your own against the better ones. Neither side is vulnerable when you see me pick up:

♠ A 7 6 5   ♡ K 10 5 4   ◇ 9 4   ♣ A 9 7

South, the dealer on my right, opens 4♠. I, after the statutory ten second pause following a jump bid in duplicate, pass. It is no surprise when North also passes but my partner, Graham, reopens with a double. I am not quite sure whether to describe this double as 'takeout' or 'optional'. With a balanced or semi-balanced hand, he expects me to pass. I only bid in the belief that we can make what I bid or, exceptionally, because we seem to have a cheap sacrifice. This hand gives me an easy decision to pass:

WEST	NORTH	EAST	SOUTH
			4♠
pass	pass	dbl	all pass

Partner's double (with my values) make most leads look reasonably safe. I settle for a boring fourth-best heart. This dummy appears:

♠ Q
♡ J 9 3
◇ J 10 6 3 2
♣ K 10 8 3

♠ A 7 6 5
♡ K 10 5 4
◇ 9 4
♣ A 9 7

```
        N
    W       E
        S
```

Partner wins with the ace, as declarer, the female half of a husband and wife partnership, plays the six. Graham returns the ♡2 to South's queen and my king wins. What do you think I should lead next?

Given that declarer has seven or eight spades to Graham's one or none, and that in theory he could cope with a 5♡ bid from me, I can read his ♡2 as his original fourth best. In this case, continuing hearts is not a good idea, as it would let declarer discard a loser on the ♡J.

One thing that strikes me is that partner would probably have cashed a top diamond if he held them both, so I place South with one of them. This figures to be the king because Graham's double is already looking a bit thin. Assuming that he has no values in spades (and indeed he may well be void in the suit), the most he can have is 13 points (♡A, ◇A-Q, ♣Q-J). A diamond lead would also be risky because declarer may not be able to score her ◇K unless we lead the suit with dummy so short of entries.

I decide to cash the ♠A on the basis that I shall have to play it on the first round of trumps anyway to stop the ♠Q from providing an entry to dummy. Partner discards the ♣5, which in our methods is a neutral card. (We play that an odd card is not encouraging in the suit discarded and may suggest the other suit of the same color — spades!).

```
                    ♠ —
                    ♡ J
                    ◇ J 10 6 3 2
                    ♣ K 10 8 3
    ♠ 7 6 5        ┌─────────────┐
    ♡ 10 5         │      N      │
    ◇ 9 4          │  W       E  │
    ♣ A 9 7        │      S      │
                   └─────────────┘
```

If declarer is 8-2-1-2, or in other words if her ◇K is a singleton, we can score three tricks in the majors and two aces in the minors for 300. If we were desperate for 500, I could underlead the ♣A in the hope Graham has the queen of clubs without the jack. However, he has already done quite well to double and South seems more likely to be 8-2-2-1. In this case, we have a chance for 500 if we defend carefully.

Since I do not want to find myself endplayed later, I cash the ♣A and exit with a trump. Although declarer runs a few trumps, Graham hangs on to his ◇A-Q and we take the last two tricks. This was the full deal:

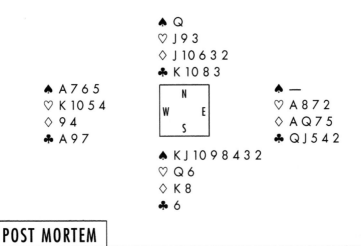

```
                    ♠ Q
                    ♡ J 9 3
                    ◇ J 10 6 3 2
                    ♣ K 10 8 3
  ♠ A 7 6 5      ┌─────────┐      ♠ —
  ♡ K 10 5 4    │    N     │      ♡ A 8 7 2
  ◇ 9 4         │ W     E  │      ◇ A Q 7 5
  ♣ A 9 7       │    S     │      ♣ Q J 5 4 2
                 └─────────┘
                    ♠ K J 10 9 8 4 3 2
                    ♡ Q 6
                    ◇ K 8
                    ♣ 6
```

POST MORTEM

'I did think about playing a club at Trick 2, to make sure you didn't either duck or underlead your ♣A,' Graham comments. 'It looked like it would help more to give you a count on the heart suit. There was also the outside chance that you had led from three hearts to the queen. The other thing I thought about was discarding the ♣Q on the ♠A, but at that point the position of the ♣A was unclear,' he adds.

This was the position after two rounds of hearts and one of spades:

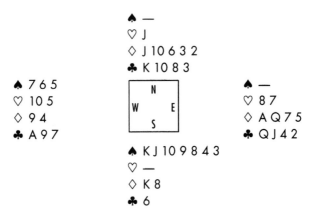

```
                    ♠ —
                    ♡ J
                    ◇ J 10 6 3 2
                    ♣ K 10 8 3
  ♠ 7 6 5       ┌─────────┐      ♠ —
  ♡ 10 5        │    N     │      ♡ 8 7
  ◇ 9 4         │ W     E  │      ◇ A Q 7 5
  ♣ A 9 7       │    S     │      ♣ Q J 4 2
                 └─────────┘
                    ♠ K J 10 9 8 4 3
                    ♡ —
                    ◇ K 8
                    ♣ 6
```

If West mistakenly leads a low club, then dummy's ♣K and ♡J score and we collect a mere 100. It is a similar story on a heart exit — the ♡J provides a discard for declarer's club loser and an entry for leading up to her ◇K.

At a key stage of a match against unfamiliar opponents, I pick up:

♠ 10 4   ♡ Q J 10 9 6 4   ◊ 8   ♣ A Q J 7

They are vulnerable and we are not. I am the dealer. How many hearts would you suggest opening?

On the losing trick count, I have six losers, making the hand far too good for a weak two (or Multi). 4♡ is out as well because I never open at the four-level on a six-card suit. This leaves the choice between 1♡ and 3♡. Using the HLQT method (see 'Strange Situation' on page 122), I count 10 points in high cards, ten cards in hearts and clubs, and one and a half defensive tricks. This totals twenty one and a half — enough for 1♡ non-vulnerable.

North doubles and East bids 1♠. South jumps to 3NT to end the bidding:

WEST	NORTH	EAST	SOUTH
1♡	dbl	1♠	3NT
all pass			

I wonder if I shall regret not having opened 3♡. It sounds as though the opponents have 12-13 points each and might have been shut out. At least the lead is very easy, the ♡Q, and this dummy comes down:

```
            ♠ A 9 8 2
            ♡ 8 2
            ◊ A K J 7
            ♣ 9 6 3
♠ 10 4          ┌───────┐
♡ Q J 10 9 6 4  │   N   │
◊ 8             │ W   E │
♣ A Q J 7       │   S   │
                └───────┘
```

Partner plays low and declarer, a middle-aged man with wavy hair, wins with the ace. He plays a diamond to the ace and my partner, Lawrence, follows with the two (standard count). The ◊K comes next, on which partner plays the six, and I discard the ♡6. The ◊J comes after that and partner plays the four. Clearly, since South began with ◇Q-x-x-x-x, I shall need to find three further discards. What do you think they should be?

I start by counting declarer's tricks: one spade at least, probably two hearts (partner would have overtaken the first heart if holding the ♡K and South would hardly leap to 3NT with only one stopper) and five diamonds. This dictates placing partner with the ♠K or declarer has nine tricks on top. Partner's ◇6 on the second round of diamonds, which is probably a suit-preference for spades, appears to confirm the location of the ♠K.

Although one cannot place the ♣K and the ♠Q for certain, can you guess where they are? With ♠Q-x in hand, declarer might well have tried to set up the queen whilst dummy still had a diamond entry. If East has the ♠Q and the ♠K, South needs the ♣K for her jump to 3NT. Putting declarer with the ♣K makes the picture clearer: I must retain two spades to avoid the danger that she might cash the ♠A and ♡K and throw me in with the third round of hearts. Accordingly, I discard the ♡4.

On the next diamond partner discards the ♠7 (high encouraging) and South overtakes. I let go the ♣7 and declarer plays her last diamond.

```
                    ♠ A 9 8 2
                    ♡ 8
                    ◇ —
                    ♣ 9 6 3
      ♠ 10 4          ┌─────────┐
      ♡ J 10 9        │    N    │
      ◇ —             │ W     E │
      ♣ A Q J         │    S    │
                      └─────────┘
```

I must still keep two spades to avoid the throw-in. It also appears that I need to save two clubs, or declarer might set up her ♣K by ducking two rounds of clubs if her shape is 2-3-5-3. Therefore, another heart goes.

Declarer continues with the ♡K, to which all follow, and a low heart. I win, as North discards a club and East a spade, and then lead the ♠10. Dummy plays low and partner wins with the ♠Q before switching to the ♣10. Declarer looks at this closely before ducking; I must overtake.

There are three spades and three clubs missing at this point, and it is hard to believe that partner has bared his ♠K to keep two low clubs. Still, since it costs nothing to cater for that possibility, I lay down the ♣A. The king does not fall and I exit with a spade to dummy's ace. Partner's ♠K takes the last trick to set the contract, with the full deal as follows:

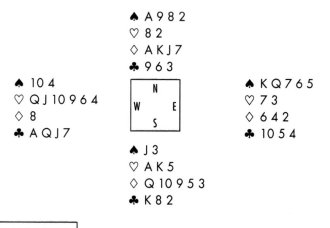

```
                    ♠ A 9 8 2
                    ♡ 8 2
                    ◇ A K J 7
                    ♣ 9 6 3
  ♠ 10 4                              ♠ K Q 7 6 5
  ♡ Q J 10 9 6 4     N                ♡ 7 3
  ◇ 8            W       E            ◇ 6 4 2
  ♣ A Q J 7          S                ♣ 10 5 4
                    ♠ J 3
                    ♡ A K 5
                    ◇ Q 10 9 5 3
                    ♣ K 8 2
```

POST MORTEM

The presence of the ♣9 in dummy saved me from having to think whether to throw the ♣Q (and keep ♣A-J-x). That would allow us to make three club tricks quickly if partner, with ♣10-9-x, could switch to the ♣10.

This was the position after one round of hearts and four of diamonds:

```
                    ♠ A 9 8 2
                    ♡ 8
                    ◇ —
                    ♣ 9 6 3
  ♠ 10 4                              ♠ K Q 6 5
  ♡ J 10 9        N                   ♡ 7
  ◇ —          W       E              ◇ —
  ♣ A Q J          S                  ♣ 10 5 4
                    ♠ J 3
                    ♡ K 5
                    ◇ Q
                    ♣ K 8 2
```

A spade or club discard by West here would concede the contract.

Swiss Teams events are popular in the UK. We normally have 20 victory points at stake in each match and the possibility of ending with two or three maximums means that many teams can stay in contention well into the event. In North America it seems to be more common to play that you just win, lose or draw, with the victory margin largely irrelevant.

Playing the last round on table three, and knowing that 20-0 would give us first place if the results on the top two tables are close, I pick up:

♠ — ♡ A K 10 3 ◇ A K 10 3 2 ♣ Q 8 4 3

The hand on my right opens 1♠ in third seat. We are all vulnerable and I double. North raises to 4♠ and two passes follow. Although 4♠ might make, a 3-2-2-6 yarborough opposite makes 5♣ a very good contract, so I double again in the hope that partner takes it out. In practice, however, this ends the auction:

WEST	NORTH	EAST	SOUTH
	pass	pass	1♠
dbl	4♠	pass	pass
dbl	all pass		

I lead the ◇ A and this is what we see:

♠ A Q J 5 3
♡ 5 2
◇ Q 8 4
♣ J 10 2

♠ —
♡ A K 10 3
◇ A K 10 3 2
♣ Q 8 4 3

```
        N
    W       E
        S
```

My partner, Andrew, follows with the ◇7 and declarer with the jack. Since the ◇Q is on view in dummy, partner's seven is a count signal, clearly implying an even number.

Declarer, a wily competitor, might have dropped the jack from J-x-x but, on this occasion, there is no reason to rush the decision. I can try a high heart next and, if partner discourages hearts, revert to diamonds. Since one can generally assume that any ace led other than on the first trick might be unsupported, I switch to the ♡K. Andrew produces the eight and South the four.

The ♡8 might be low from J-9-8 but the chances seem good that it is an encouraging card. Do you think I should play partner for the ♡Q or a doubleton? Well, even with only one diamond, the odds must be against finding declarer with 5-5 in the majors. I could try to hedge my bets by cashing the ♡A next but, if declarer holds ♡J-x-x-x, partner's queen will come down on the third round and one of dummy's clubs could go away on the ♡J. Since, with only one diamond trick, we presumably need two hearts and a club to defeat the contract, I do not wish this to happen. After saying a little prayer, I continue with the ♡3.

Somebody must have heard because partner wins with the queen. He thinks for a while and then switches to the ♣6. Maybe he took my ♡3 as suit-preference for clubs, although a club switch looks attractive anyway in view of dummy's holding. Declarer rises with the ace and then plays three rounds of trumps. I have to find three discards in this position:

```
              ♠ A Q J 5 3
              ♡ —
              ◇ Q 8
              ♣ J 10
♠ —                      ┌─────────┐
♡ A 10                   │    N    │
◇ K 10 3 2            W  │       E │
♣ Q 8 3                  │    S    │
                         └─────────┘
```

Fortunately, this does not present too much difficulty. I must keep two diamonds so that declarer cannot set up dummy's ◇Q for a club discard by ruffing a diamond in hand. Likewise, it is necessary to keep two hearts in case declarer has two hearts instead. I therefore throw two diamonds and one club. Partner follows to all three spades and declarer predictably ruffs a diamond in hand and a heart in dummy.

I still have the ♡A and ◇K left and, when declarer's last effort is to run the ♣J, my ♣Q takes the setting trick. This was the full deal:

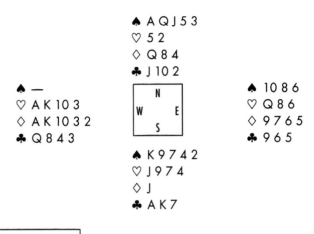

Clearly any lead other than the ♡3 at the third trick would prove
fatal: a diamond would have set up the queen, a club would be into
a tenace and the ♡10 would set up a ruffing finesse. Less obvious,
maybe, is East's role. See what happens if he plays back a diamond
instead of the club. After the switch back to diamonds, declarer
ruffs two diamonds and draws trumps to leave dummy on lead in
this position:

```
              ♠ J 5
              ♡ —
              ◇ —
              ♣ J 10 2
    ♠ —       ┌─────────┐      ♠ —
    ♡ A 10    │    N    │      ♡ 6
    ◇ —       │ W     E │      ◇ 9
    ♣ Q 8 3   │    S    │      ♣ 9 6 5
              └─────────┘
              ♠ —
              ♡ J 9
              ◇ —
              ♣ A K 7
```

What would you suggest throwing on the next spade if declarer discards the ♣7? If I let go a club, cashing the ♣A-K leaves dummy
high. If I part with a heart, a club to the ace and a heart ruff leaves
the South hand high.

Gaping Jaws 46

At the end of a session's bridge, I usually recall one or two deals on which it was not clear whether the contract was makeable with correct play on both sides. It is then great fun entering the deals in a brilliant piece of software called *Deep Finesse*. This tells you at any point whether the given contract is on and which are the winning and losing cards to play. In conjunction with an invaluable related program called *Dealmaster Pro*, it also helps me when I need to give a commentary on a set of deals. Of course, sometimes you have little hope of finding the best double-dummy line at the table. Then again, sometimes you just might...

Take these East cards as dealer with neither side vulnerable:

♠ Q 4   ♡ 8 7   ◇ K J 9 7 6 4 2   ♣ 6 3

You open 3◇ but the opponents reach 4♠ as follows:

WEST	NORTH	EAST	SOUTH
		3◇	3♠
4◇	dbl	pass	4♠
all pass			

Partner leads the ace of hearts and dummy puts down this:

♠ 8 3
♡ Q 9 6 5 4
◇ A Q
♣ Q 8 7 2

	N	
W		E
	S	

East:
♠ Q 4
♡ 8 7
◇ K J 9 7 6 4 2
♣ 6 3

You follow with the ♡8, naturally enough, and declarer drops the ♡J.

Partner, who you can assume is a good player, continues with the king of hearts. Declarer plays the three and, when partner continues with the ♡10, covers with dummy's queen. First, how high do you ruff this third heart?

Generally, if you might be overruffed and think there is a chance of promoting a trump trick for partner, you ruff high. As against that, if South has a third heart, you may not want to waste the queen. Which is it to be?

With these East cards, it would occur to me that my queen cannot usefully cover anything in dummy. This means that it can hardly cost to ruff high. Let us say you do ruff high and South throws a club. What do you propose to do next? These are the cards left on view:

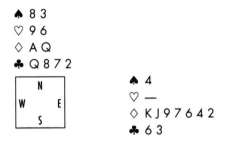

♠ 8 3
♡ 9 6
◇ A Q
♣ Q 8 7 2

♠ 4
♡ —
◇ K J 9 7 6 4 2
♣ 6 3

Partner might hold a trump trick or declarer the ace-king of clubs, in which case your return does not matter. The 'obvious' suit to lead is clubs, up to the weakness, and partner's possible ♣A might run away if South holds a seven-card spade suit.

Of course, you know in a problem not to expect the obvious. I think you could also solve this at the table. There are three clues, all in the same direction. Firstly, if holding the ♣A, why did partner not cash it before playing the third heart? Secondly, and more significantly, why would anyone wanting to give a suit-preference signal for clubs play the ♡10 on the third round rather than the ♡2? Thirdly, if the ♣A is out, might declarer not overruff the heart and try to play trumps without loss?

Surely, declarer has the ♣A and will happily win a club switch, draw trumps, cross to the ◇A and run the hearts. The solution is simple once you think of it. Return a diamond, yes, giving declarer two diamond tricks instead of one. However, the trick comes back with interest. Now dummy makes no heart tricks (because you can ruff) and the ♣K with partner will normally suffice to defeat the contract. Here is the full deal:

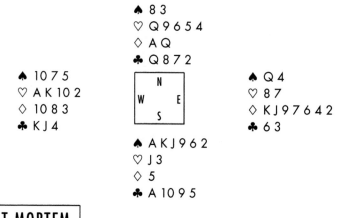

```
                    ♠ 8 3
                    ♡ Q 9 6 5 4
                    ◇ A Q
                    ♣ Q 8 7 2
  ♠ 10 7 5          ┌─────────┐          ♠ Q 4
  ♡ A K 10 2        │    N    │          ♡ 8 7
  ◇ 10 8 3          │  W   E  │          ◇ K J 9 7 6 4 2
  ♣ K J 4           │    S    │          ♣ 6 3
                    └─────────┘
                    ♠ A K J 9 6 2
                    ♡ J 3
                    ◇ 5
                    ♣ A 10 9 5
```

POST MORTEM

This deal was unusual in that the sacrifice of a trick in diamonds
was quite genuine. The trick came back because it killed two heart
winners. More common perhaps is the situation in which declarer
cannot take advantage of the extra winner, often because a defender can ruff, as here:

```
                    ♠ K Q 8 3
                    ♡ 9 5
                    ◇ 9 5 3
                    ♣ A Q 10 5
  ♠ 10 9 6 4 2      ┌─────────┐          ♠ A J 7
  ♡ 8 3            │    N    │          ♡ A 4
  ◇ 8 7 6 2         │  W   E  │          ◇ Q J 10
  ♣ 9 4            │    S    │          ♣ K J 8 6 3
                    └─────────┘
                    ♠ 5
                    ♡ K Q J 10 7 6 2
                    ◇ A K 4
                    ♣ 7 2
```

South, who has shown a long strong heart suit and better than a minimum opening bid, plays in 4♡. West finds the best lead, the ♣9, clearly
top of a doubleton or possibly a singleton, and this goes to the ten and
jack. East, judging that West is unlikely to hold one of the top diamonds,
should return a club into the ace-queen. This removes the entry to
dummy's spade winner and defeats the contract. A mistaken switch to
the ◇Q would allow declarer to win and immediately knock out the ace
of spades, the ♣A being the entry to enjoy the established winner.

My brother John once gave me a book with these words inscribed: 'When the great scorer comes, it matters not whether you won or lost but how you played the game.' I can readily relate to those words. Nobody likes to lose a match but it can make the pain easier to bear if the answer is yes to the question 'Have I played my best?' and no to the question 'Did I let the team down?'

In a match, in fourth seat with the other side vulnerable, I hold:

♠ Q J 6 4 ♡ 7 2 ◇ Q 9 ♣ A K J 9 4

After 1♡, pass, 1♠, I think the hand easily justifies a 2♣ overcall despite the lack of a sixth club. The bidding continues as follows:

WEST	NORTH	EAST	SOUTH
			1♡
pass	1♠	2♣	2◇
pass	4♡	all pass	

John, my partner, leads the ♣6 and this is what we see:

```
            ♠ A K 10 3
            ♡ Q J 4
            ◇ J 6 4
            ♣ Q 10 3
         ┌─────────┐
         │    N    │      ♠ Q J 6 4
         │ W     E │      ♡ 7 2
         │    S    │      ◇ Q 9
         └─────────┘      ♣ A K J 9 4
```

Dummy plays the ♣10 and I win with the jack. South, Elizabeth, one of the stronger players on their team, follows with the seven.

The ♣6 lead is consistent with a holding of 8-6-5-2 and partner may be too weak (or too flat) to have raised my clubs. Even so, I see no urgency to switch and return the king. South follows with five and partner follows upwards with the eight, which makes the club position clear.

With only two club tricks possible, it occurs to me that for us to defeat the contract, partner will need a fast red winner and control of the fourth round of diamonds. I am not quite sure whether to play trumps. Although I cannot overruff the ♡Q or ♡J in dummy on the fourth round, maybe declarer will give me the chance to ruff dummy's ◇J on the third.

Since declarer would not have much of an opening bid without the ◇A, I am about to try the ◇Q when it strikes me that she might win, draw a round of trumps and lead towards the jack. If John can go in with the king and give me a ruff, she might have had two diamond losers anyway.

It seems right to go back to my initial thought of switching to a trump, and dummy's queen wins. Declarer, who knows that I would cover the ◇J with ◇K-x-(x) or ◇Q-x-(x), tries a low diamond off dummy instead. What would you suggest doing here?

```
            ♠ A K 10 3
            ♡ J 4
            ◇ J 6 4
            ♣ Q
        ┌─────────┐      ♠ Q J 6 4
        │    N    │      ♡ 7
        │ W     E │      ◇ Q 9
        │    S    │      ♣ A 9 4
        └─────────┘
```

If John has ◇K-10-x-x, then we have nothing to fear. What if declarer has ◇A-10-x-x? If I play low, she may finesse the ten, which John will win. If John does not return a trump himself, she can draw a second round when she gets in. Then nothing can stop her from cashing the ◇J and later ruffing the fourth round of diamonds in dummy. Could putting up the queen disrupt this plan? Yes, declarer will have to take her ace and, if she plays a second round of diamonds, John can give me a ruff. If, instead, she draws a second round of trumps, John will be able to play a third round when he gets in. I do play the ◇Q and declarer does play the ◇A. After a few moment's thought, she decides to draw the missing trumps. John eventually scores two diamond tricks because this was the full deal:

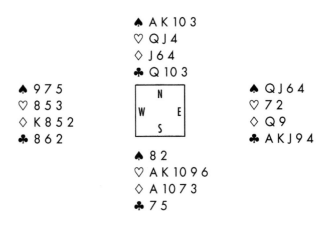

```
              ♠ A K 10 3
              ♡ Q J 4
              ◇ J 6 4
              ♣ Q 10 3
♠ 9 7 5          N          ♠ Q J 6 4
♡ 8 5 3     W        E      ♡ 7 2
◇ K 8 5 2        S          ◇ Q 9
♣ 8 6 2                     ♣ A K J 9 4
              ♠ 8 2
              ♡ A K 10 9 6
              ◇ A 10 7 3
              ♣ 7 5
```

POST MORTEM

Declarer's aim was to draw exactly two rounds of trumps. The counter was for East to play high in second seat so that West could win the second diamond, threatening to give East a ruff. More commonly, the defenders would thwart an ambition to draw precisely two rounds of trumps with the play of a high card in the trump suit itself.

```
              ♡ 10 9 4
♡ K 5 3                      ♡ Q 2
              ♡ A J 8 7 6
```

With this trump layout, declarer plans to finesse the ♡J and repeat the finesse after getting the lead back in dummy. This will leave one trump in dummy and one defender out of trumps. Perhaps it will then be safe to ruff something in dummy. In order to scotch that plan, East hops up with the queen when a low trump comes off dummy. Declarer now has two choices: duck and lose two tricks as the cards lie, or win and allow West to win the second round with the king and play the third round.

$\heartsuit$ 10 9 4

$\heartsuit$ 5 3 ⬜ $\heartsuit$ K Q 2

$\heartsuit$ A J 8 7 6

Assuming the bidding does not mark East with the K-Q, playing the queen (or king) on the first round should prove effective here as well. Rather than lose two tricks if East actually had Q-x or K-x, declarer figures to take the ace. This way East can win the second round and play a third.

Anything You Can Do

48

Many people know that, if declarer has a holding something like A-9-x-x facing K-10-x-x in a side suit, the defenders should avoid leading the suit, especially if one of them has the queen and the other jack. They may do better to lead another suit even if it means conceding a ruff and discard. This advice can, of course, apply on a number of other layouts.

Our opponents have asked for a practice session before the Summer Nationals and, with our side vulnerable, I pick up this:

♠ K 5   ♡ 8 2   ◇ K 10 5 4   ♣ K Q J 7 5

In third seat I open 1♣. Marc on my left overcalls 1NT, my partner, David, passes and Peter on my right bids 2◇, a transfer. Marc completes the transfer and, when offered a choice of games, converts to 4♡:

WEST	NORTH	EAST	SOUTH
		1♣	1NT
pass	2◇	pass	2♡
pass	3NT	pass	4♡
all pass			

Partner leads the ♣4 and this is what comes down in dummy:

```
            ♠ Q 9 2
            ♡ Q J 9 6 5
            ◇ A J 9
            ♣ 8 6
        ┌─────────┐
        │    N    │        ♠ K 5
        │ W     E │        ♡ 8 2
        │    S    │        ◇ K 10 5 4
        └─────────┘        ♣ K Q J 7 5
```

I put up the ♣J, which holds, declarer playing the three. I return the king, which the ace captures, and partner follows upwards with the nine.

Declarer leads the ♣10 and ruffs it in dummy before playing the ♡Q. If this is a finesse, that suits me fine, but it wins. Next comes a heart to the ace and a diamond to the two, nine and ten. This is what we see left:

```
        ♠ Q 9 2
        ♡ J 9
        ◇ A J
        ♣ —
    ┌─────────┐      ♠ K 5
    │    N    │      ♡ —
    │ W     E │      ◇ K 5 4
    │    S    │      ♣ Q 7
    └─────────┘
```

What do we know about the strength of the unseen hands?
Declarer started with at least 15 points and the ♡A-K and the ♣A
have already appeared. To make up his points he must have the
♠A. I can also place the ◇Q. Finessing dummy's ◇9 would make
no sense unless David, my partner, holds this card. Although the
position of the ♠J is less clear, David must have it if we are to stand
a chance of beating the contract.

What can we tell about the distribution? Three rounds of clubs
have gone and West and South started with three each. Partner's
◇2 looks like the bottom of a three-card holding, though arguably
he might not put up the queen from a doubleton Q-2. Knowing
Marc's bidding style, he would not worry too much about the lack
of a diamond stopper and would only take himself out of 3NT if he
has either four trumps or three trumps and a ruffing value. Since he
appears to be 3-3 in the minors and so lacks a ruffing value, I read
him for a 3-4-3-3 shape.

At first sight, it looks right to return the ◇K, to allow partner to
win the third round of diamonds and lead a spade through
dummy's queen. A moment's reflection, however, shows the risk in
this. If partner has the ♠J but not the ♠10, declarer will play low
from dummy on his spade exit. Then, whether I play high or low,
declarer can play the spades for three tricks. Partner, with only
spades left, will have no choice in the matter. I, by contrast, will
have spare cards in the minors to lead. True, leading one means giving up a ruff and discard, but we will still make a spade trick. I
carry out my plan, returning the ◇4 now and playing a club when
in with the ◇K. Later I cover the ♠Q and the contract goes down.
This was the full deal:

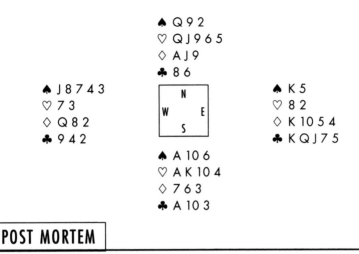

```
              ♠ Q 9 2
              ♡ Q J 9 6 5
              ◇ A J 9
              ♣ 8 6
♠ J 8 7 4 3          N          ♠ K 5
♡ 7 3          W           E    ♡ 8 2
◇ Q 8 2              S          ◇ K 10 5 4
♣ 9 4 2                         ♣ K Q J 7 5
              ♠ A 10 6
              ♡ A K 10 4
              ◇ 7 6 3
              ♣ A 10 3
```

POST MORTEM

If South had held a 2-4-4-3 shape, it would have been better to return a low diamond rather than the king. Yes, but the odds were roughly 4 to 1 that the ◇2 was not partner's only low diamond. This was the end position:

```
              ♠ Q 9 2
              ♡ J 9
              ◇ A J
              ♣ —
♠ J 8 7 4 3          N          ♠ K 5
♡ —            W           E    ♡ —
◇ Q 2                S          ◇ K 5 4
♣ —                             ♣ Q 7
              ♠ A 10 6
              ♡ K 10
              ◇ 7 3
              ♣ —
```

We needed to defend as we did here to beat the contract. Please take note of this spade layout, and of the one below. Again the defenders should be loath to touch this even if it means giving a ruff and discard.

```
        ♠ K 9 7
♠ Q 6 5 4 2  ┌───┐  ♠ A 10
             └───┘
        ♠ J 8 3
```

Dynamic Duo

49

In the UK and elsewhere, many players like simultaneous pairs events. Whether worldwide or restricted to one country, county or continent, they offer you several things. Without going beyond your local club, you can compete against many others and see your scores on the Internet. If you do well, you may collect loads of masterpoints. Lastly, and by no means least, you invariably receive a booklet with hand records and a helpful commentary. True, you might get hand records on ordinary club nights with a Duplimate machine but few clubs can afford to invest in one.

During one such event, this shapely collection comes my way:

$$\spadesuit — \quad \heartsuit\,A\,K\,J\,7\,6\,5 \quad \diamondsuit\,Q\,9\,6\,3 \quad \clubsuit\,Q\,J\,4$$

With neither side vulnerable, North opens 1♣ and I overcall 1♡. South bids 1♠, showing a five-card suit because they play negative doubles. West passes and North's jump to 4♠ concludes the bidding:

WEST	NORTH	EAST	SOUTH
	1♣	1♡	1♠
pass	4♠	all pass	

My partner, John, leads the ♡9 and this strong dummy appears:

```
            ♠ A K 10 4
            ♡ Q 2
            ◊ A K 8
            ♣ K 9 6 5
          ┌─────────┐
          │    N    │      ♠ —
          │ W     E │      ♡ A K J 7 6 5
          │    S    │      ◊ Q 9 6 3
          └─────────┘      ♣ Q J 4
```

Dummy plays low and I win with the jack as South plays the three. My next play is easy, cashing the ♡K, and this collects the eight, four and queen. We sometimes play 'strong ten' leads (in which case the ten would promise an interior sequence and the nine could come from 10-9-x) but not in suit contracts. Thus South must hold the missing heart.

My next play does not seem difficult either. A diamond switch might cost a trick unless partner has the jack and a club switch might cost a trick if South has ♣A-10-x. By contrast, a third heart cannot cost, and forcing the dummy might make it difficult to pick up West's trumps. Partner discards the ◇5, which, given that the ◇2 and ◇4 are missing, looks neutral (we play revolving discards).

After ruffing in dummy, declarer cashes the ♠A and I throw a low heart whilst partner follows with the two. Next come the ace, king and a third round of diamonds. South, who started with ◇J-x, ruffs the third round and John makes a gentle high-low with the four and two. After this comes a low trump, which goes to the five and ten, and I discard a heart. Next declarer leads a low club off dummy. This is what we can see left:

```
          ♠ K
          ♡ —
          ◇ —
          ♣ K 9 6 5
       ┌─────────┐
       │    N    │      ♠ —
       │ W     E │      ♡ 7
       │    S    │      ◇ 6
       └─────────┘      ♣ Q J 4
```

It must be right to play the jack (or queen) to stop declarer from winning cheaply with the ten or, if John has this card, to leave myself with the option of unblocking. The ♣A wins, John playing the three, and back comes the ♣8, on which he plays the seven, to dummy's king.

There are three possibilities here: (i) if John has ♠Q-J or ♠Q-9 and no ♣10, I should play low and wait for us to score a trump and a club; (ii) if John has neither the ♣10 nor a possible trump trick, I should play low to stop the overtrick (a factor at matchpoints); (iii) if South has ♠J-9 but not the ♣10, I need to unblock or my forced red-suit return will smother John's ♠Q. It is easy to dismiss half of (i) straight away. John would hardly have let dummy's ♠10 score if he held ♠Q-J. (ii) also seems unlikely; in that case declarer is playing a deep game; it would seem far more normal to run the trumps and hope for a squeeze. A further clue is that John might have thrown a club on the third heart if all his clubs were low.

What are the odds if we ignore John's discard? His low-high in clubs and the rest of the play gives us a count: South began with

5-3 in the black suits and West 4-3. We also 'know', for it to matter, that South has the ♠J, West the ♠Q, and South has played the ♣A. This means South began with four of the seven low spades and West with three out of the five low clubs. This makes the odds four to three that South has the ♠9 and three to two that West has the ♣10, making my (iii) roughly twice as likely as (i). I unblock and am pleased to find that the full deal is:

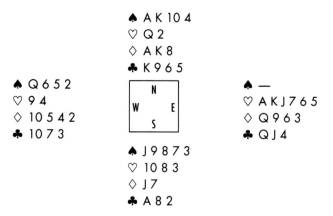

```
                    ♠ A K 10 4
                    ♡ Q 2
                    ◇ A K 8
                    ♣ K 9 6 5
  ♠ Q 6 5 2          ┌─────────┐          ♠ —
  ♡ 9 4              │    N    │          ♡ A K J 7 6 5
  ◇ 10 5 4 2         │ W     E │          ◇ Q 9 6 3
  ♣ 10 7 3           │    S    │          ♣ Q J 4
                     └─────────┘
                    ♠ J 9 8 7 3
                    ♡ 10 8 3
                    ◇ J 7
                    ♣ A 8 2
```

POST MORTEM

This would have been the end position if East failed to unblock:

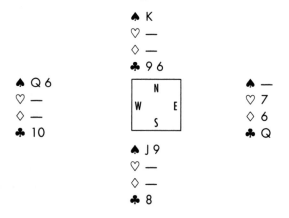

```
                    ♠ K
                    ♡ —
                    ◇ —
                    ♣ 9 6
  ♠ Q 6              ┌─────────┐          ♠ —
  ♡ —               │    N    │          ♡ 7
  ◇ —               │ W     E │          ◇ 6
  ♣ 10              │    S    │          ♣ Q
                     └─────────┘
                    ♠ J 9
                    ♡ —
                    ◇ —
                    ♣ 8
```

After winning the third round of clubs, East must return a red card. Declarer ruffs and the ♠Q bites the dust whether or not West overruffs.

Bridge bidding theory has, for me, two big paradoxes. The first concerns opening bids. Why do some open a four-card major, even with quite a weak suit, whilst others never open 1♡ or 1♠ on four no matter what the circumstances? After all, when it comes to overcalls, some consensus exists that one might overcall on a four-card suit. Although I do not have the definitive book on the subject, *The Complete Book of Overcalls* by Mike Lawrence, to hand, my requirements very likely resemble his. These are: a strong suit that you can show at the one-level, opening values, and a hand unsuited for a takeout double or 1NT overcall.

The second concerns 1NT openings and rebids. Some players open 1NT with a good five-card major or, though not with five spades and four hearts, on a 5422 type. I have no problem with that. What mystifies me is that some of the same players elect to open 1♣ and rebid 1♡ or 1♠ with a 4333 type. Surely, if you believe that showing your hand type and range takes precedence over finding a fit quickly, you should apply that principle whether you are choosing an opening or a rebid.

In this match I have agreed to play Acol with a strong notrump throughout and pick up:

♠ J 8 6 5   ♡ A Q 8   ◇ J 10 3   ♣ K J 4

If we were vulnerable, I might well pass. As it is, I open 1♣, intending to rebid 1NT, but the bidding goes like this:

WEST	NORTH	EAST	SOUTH
		1♣	1♠
pass	2◇	pass	2NT
pass	3NT	all pass	

Partner leads the ♣7 and this 2-4-5-2 twelve-count comes down:

```
            ♠ 10 3
            ♡ K 10 7 4
            ◇ A K 8 6 2
            ♣ Q 10
        ┌───────────┐        ♠ J 8 6 5
        │     N     │        ♡ A Q 8
        │  W     E  │        ◇ J 10 3
        │     S     │        ♣ K J 4
        └───────────┘
```

Dummy plays the ♣10 and I play the jack. This wins when declarer, a man about my own age, follows with the two. I return the king of clubs, which also wins when South plays the three and West the five. I continue with the ♣4 and this time declarer takes the ace. West follows with the six and dummy discards a low heart. Since my partner, David, regards the normal carding with four low cards to be the second highest followed by the lowest, he does not mean his ♣5 (from ♣9-7-6-5) as suit-preference.

I expect declarer to play on diamonds, probably by ducking a trick into my hand so West cannot get in to cash his ♣9 and lead a heart through dummy's king. This prediction is half right. Declarer attacks diamonds, playing the ace, king and another. West, who turns up with ◇Q-9 alone, discards the ♡6 on third round. How do you suggest I continue?

<pre>
            ♠ 10 3
            ♡ K 10 7
            ◇ 8 6
            ♣ —
        ┌─────────┐   ♠ J 8 6 5
        │   N   │   ♡ A Q 8
        │ W   E │   ◇ —
        │   S   │   ♣ —
        └─────────┘
</pre>

The 'natural' play here is a low spade. If declarer takes the ace, king and queen (and that is assuming partner has none of these cards), I have the fourth round covered. The sole danger is that declarer might let the lead run around to the ten. Do you think this can really happen?

Given my opening bid and the fact that I have only produced 5 points so far, declarer may be able to count me for the ♠J. Even if not, he may have no choice if his spades are A-K-Q-x; they would certainly be good enough for an overcall. Indeed, given that David would hardly discard the ♡6 (i.e. starting a high-low) from a five-card suit, one has reason to put South with a 4-2-3-4 shape.

Prospects suddenly seem less rosy. Since any exit will concede both a trick and an entry to dummy, it looks like nine tricks will make. Luckily, I spot that leading the *jack* of spades can foul up the works. If dummy wins the second spade, declarer cannot cash his last two spades. If he wins it in hand, the long diamonds are dead.

This is the full deal:

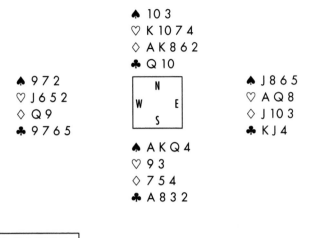

```
                    ♠ 10 3
                    ♡ K 10 7 4
                    ◇ A K 8 6 2
                    ♣ Q 10
   ♠ 9 7 2                        ♠ J 8 6 5
   ♡ J 6 5 2         N            ♡ A Q 8
   ◇ Q 9         W       E        ◇ J 10 3
   ♣ 9 7 6 5         S            ♣ K J 4
                    ♠ A K Q 4
                    ♡ 9 3
                    ◇ 7 5 4
                    ♣ A 8 3 2
```

POST MORTEM

If my diamonds had been Q-10-x, I would have had to consider whether to unblock on the ace and king to create an entry for partner, watching to see whether he showed an odd or even number. Unblocking might have been essential if declarer had held ♠A-K-Q-9 and only two diamonds. On my actual hand, this was the position after three rounds of each minor:

```
                    ♠ 10 3
                    ♡ K 10 7
                    ◇ 8 6
                    ♣ —
   ♠ 9 7 2                        ♠ J 8 6 5
   ♡ J 5 2           N            ♡ A Q 8
   ◇ —           W       E        ◇ —
   ♣ 9               S            ♣ —
                    ♠ A K Q 4
                    ♡ 9 3
                    ◇ —
                    ♣ 8
```

Any exit other than the ♠J allows the contract to make.

Close Double

Amongst other things, *The Notrump Zone* by Danny Kleinman discusses the merits of weak and strong 1NT openings. My view, in support of the weak variety, which virtually echoes Edgar Kaplan's, runs as follows: A 1NT opening is both descriptive and preemptive whilst an opening of one of a minor that may be short is neither. You can lose by opening a short minor if the opponents overcall at the one-level and 1NT would have shut them out. You can also lose if your suit is real but partner cannot tell.

True, occasionally you lose a big penalty getting doubled in 1NT or in your runout suit. Also, if you play weak when vulnerable at pairs, you might lose 200 undoubled (though that could happen if you open a minor and rebid 1NT or are left in a short minor). If you switch from strong to weak, you need to think how to respond to one of a suit with a good 9 or 10 points. If you bid 1NT and partner might have 15 or 16 and pass, then you miss game.

Danny tells me that he switched from strong to weak because, if you open one of minor, you can find a 4-4 fit in a major that you miss if you open 1NT and partner is too weak for Stayman. At pairs, he does not want to play in 1NT when the field is in a suit contract unless 1NT is superior.

♠ A 6 4   ♡ 10 5 3   ◇ A J 10   ♣ A Q 8 4

When I held this hand in a league match, my opponents were using weak notrumps in the simple auction below. I regard this hand as the minimum for a penalty double. 1NT contracts are notoriously difficult to defend, doubled or undoubled.

WEST	NORTH	EAST	SOUTH
			1NT
pass	pass	dbl	all pass

Partner leads the ♡4 (fourth best) and dummy puts this down:

```
                    ♠ J 10 7
                    ♡ K 8
                    ◇ K 7 6 5 4
                    ♣ J 10 9
          ┌─────────────┐
          │      N      │      ♠ A 6 4
          │ W         E │      ♡ 10 5 3
          │      S      │      ◇ A J 10
          └─────────────┘      ♣ A Q 8 4
```

Declarer, an elegant lady, plays low from dummy and takes my ♡10 with the jack. Instinctively I place her with A-J-x rather than Q-J-x: most people win with the queen from the latter holding. Of course, she cannot have a doubleton A-J because there is only one heart lower than the four missing.

Declarer leads the three of spades from hand. Partner follows with the two (standard count) and dummy puts up the jack. What would you do?

Dummy is disappointingly strong and the opening lead has hardly helped. With 8 points in dummy and at least 12 dealt to South, partner can hold at most 5. That could be a king in addition to the ♡Q. With the two red kings on view, clearly the ♣K will prove more useful than the ♠K because this will improve the value of my clubs. Even so, if I take the ♠A and we cash four club tricks, there does not appear to be any way to defeat the contract. Declarer will, after regaining the lead, be able to unblock the ♡K and make seven tricks by way of three spades, three hearts and a diamond.

I hold up the ♠A twice, winning on the third round. Partner's second spade is the five, which is pleasing, because it could be a suit-preference signal for clubs and it means South has the ♠K-Q. I switch to the ♣4 and partner produces the king. We cash four club tricks, with both opponents throwing a diamond on the fourth round. These are the cards still visible:

```
                    ♠ —
                    ♡ K
                    ◇ K 7 6 5
                    ♣ —
          ┌─────────────┐
          │      N      │      ♠ —
          │ W         E │      ♡ 5 3
          │      S      │      ◇ A J 10
          └─────────────┘      ♣ —
```

It is clear that the 'safe' lead of a heart to the king will not work. Declarer will continue with a low diamond off dummy and the ◇Q will serve as an entry to the long spade and the ♡A. Instead, I need to lead the ◇J, attacking declarer's entry to her hand. There is no risk attached to this because I have a complete count on the distribution. Declarer must have a long spade and, since the opening lead marked her with at least three hearts, she must be down to a doubleton diamond. Taking the ◇Q, she cashes the long spade and ducks a diamond, no doubt hoping my ace will appear; in practice, I cash the ◇A-10 for one down. This was the full deal:

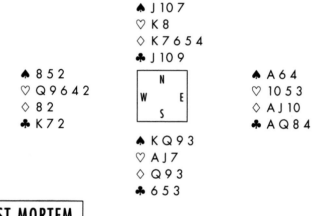

POST MORTEM

This was the position before East cashed the fourth club:

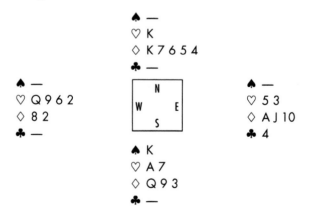

Declarer is squeezed in three suits and cannot escape.

Losing Option

Ask players the question 'what aspect of defending do you find hardest?' and many will give the same answer: 'discarding when declarer runs a long suit'. Indeed, sometimes you cannot keep all the cards you need and fall victim to a squeeze.

Fortunately, there are a number of pseudo-squeeze positions, like the one we saw in 'Blessing in Disguise', that correct discarding can defeat. You will also come across a further group of squeezes, the operation of which depends upon declarer's ability to read what the defenders have kept. This ambiguity often arises with the strip squeeze, the trump squeeze, the criss-cross squeeze and the compound squeeze. The contract usually makes in practice because the defenders discard their spare cards first and go into a long trance before parting with a vital card as their final discard. Good defenders will avoid this situation by working out what the end position will be before it arises and planning in advance what to keep.

In a league match, with both sides vulnerable, I pick up:

♠ A J 7 3   ♡ K 10 9 6 5   ◇ K 9 6   ♣ Q

Partner opens a weak 2♠ and the next player doubles. With the known ten-card fit, I jump to 4♠. True, since 3NT and 4♡ are unlikely to be on their way, there is a risk of losing 200 in 4♠ doubled on a partscore deal. Still, 4♠ might make and I want to apply maximum pressure. South, a flamboyantly dressed man, bids 5♣ and there is no further bidding:

WEST	NORTH	EAST	SOUTH
2♠	dbl	4♠	5♣
all pass			

Partner leads the ♠K and a fairly strong dummy appears:

LOSING OPTION

```
              ♠ 9 8
              ♡ A Q 8 3
              ◇ A Q 10 5 2
              ♣ A 2
                              ♠ A J 7 3
        ┌─────────┐           ♡ K 10 9 6 5
        │    N    │           ◇ K 9 6
        │ W     E │           ♣ Q
        │    S    │
        └─────────┘
```

Dummy is stronger than it might have been. However, my kings
both look well placed and a spade trick will stand up. If dummy
had the singleton spade, my signal on this first spade would be suit-
preference and the present situation seems equivalent. Having
raised spades but not doubled 5♣, partner knows that I have good
spade support. With only three spades, the onus would fall on me
to overtake the spade and return the suit. I play the ♠J, therefore,
and partner seems to get the message, switching to the ♡J. The ace
goes up and, having already asked for a heart, I have no need to
encourage and follow low.

   Declarer cashes the ♣A, to which all follow, and plays another
trump to the king. I discard a spade on this and, on the third round
of trumps, partner does likewise. These are the cards left on view
as dummy throws the ◇2:

```
              ♠ 9
              ♡ Q 8 3
              ◇ A Q 10 5 2
              ♣ —
                              ♠ A 7
        ┌─────────┐           ♡ K 10 9 6
        │    N    │           ◇ K 9 6
        │ W     E │           ♣ —
        │    S    │
        └─────────┘
```

It is certain that declarer started with eight clubs and he seems
intent on running the suit. This means I need to find six more discards and think about what three cards to keep for the ending. I
expect that dummy will keep the ace-queen of diamonds and the
queen of hearts. Of course, this will not happen if declarer is 8-1-3-1
because then he will finesse the ◇10 rather than run the trumps —
but then we can never defeat the contract.

   On the bidding, declarer cannot be sure who holds the ◇K,
although he may have a good idea. If he does intend to finesse the
◇Q, I can probably relax.

The dangerous situation is that declarer intends to exit with a heart for a return into dummy's ◊A-Q. Indeed, if he reads my exact hand, there is no effective counter. Luckily, from his point of view, partner's switch to the ♡J may look like it comes from ♡J-10-x. If I keep two hearts and one diamond, he may go wrong either by exiting with a heart, letting me cash two hearts, or by finessing into my unguarded ◊K. He may go down even if he guesses my shape (he does not know who has the ◊K) and, if he makes the contract, at least I have done my best. This is the full deal:

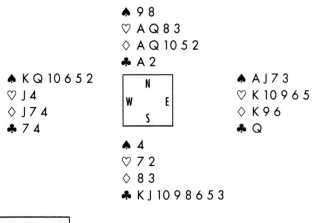

```
              ♠ 9 8
              ♡ A Q 8 3
              ◊ A Q 10 5 2
              ♣ A 2
♠ K Q 10 6 5 2        ┌─────────┐    ♠ A J 7 3
♡ J 4                 │    N    │    ♡ K 10 9 6 5
◊ J 7 4               │ W     E │    ◊ K 9 6
♣ 7 4                 │    S    │    ♣ Q
                      └─────────┘
              ♠ 4
              ♡ 7 2
              ◊ 8 3
              ♣ K J 10 9 8 6 5 3
```

POST MORTEM

An alternative strategy would be to keep a spade and both red kings, as shown below. The disadvantage is that declarer should know not to play for the throw-in and therefore has fewer ways of going wrong.

```
              ♠ —
              ♡ Q
              ◊ A Q
              ♣ —
♠ —                   ┌─────────┐    ♠ 7
♡ 4                   │    N    │    ♡ K
◊ J 7                 │ W     E │    ◊ K
♣ —                   │    S    │    ♣ —
                      └─────────┘
              ♠ —
              ♡ 7
              ◊ 8 3
              ♣ —
```

The laws of bridge as they relate to variations in tempo and unauthorized information tend to work to the benefit of the declaring side. Defenders must take care to ignore any hesitations their partners make and might have to rush some of their plays to avoid a break in tempo. Nevertheless, they can tune in on declarer's actions. As a defender, when you or your partner shows out of a suit, you can often sense whether declarer regards this as a bad break or an expected event. You can also use clues from the bidding. For example if, in the sequence 1♡-3♡-4♡, 4♡ was slow, you might infer declarer has a hand almost worth a slam try. Most people know when they open whether they think their hand is minimum.

In an inter-county teams match I pick up:

♠ A 8 7 6 4   ♡ A K 2   ◇ J 10 4   ♣ Q 7

The other side alone is vulnerable and North, the dealer, opens 1◇. I overcall 1♠ and South passes. My partner, Graham, jumps preemptively to 3♠. North seems untroubled by this and doubles for takeout. I pass and South goes into a long trance, eventually emerging with a bid of 4♡. Partner passes, which is the disciplined thing to do when your jump bid has forced the opponents to guess. I have sound values but am much too balanced to think 4♠ will make or to contemplate a sacrifice. In any case, we should stand a good chance of defeating 4♡. Indeed, a fourth heart with these values would probably justify doubling. The bidding has been:

WEST	NORTH	EAST	SOUTH
	1◇	1♠	pass
3♠	dbl	pass	4♡
all pass			

Partner leads the ♠Q and dummy is as strong as you would expect:

```
                    ♠ 9
                    ♡ Q J 8
                    ◊ A K Q 8 5 3
                    ♣ A K 9
          ┌─────────────┐      ♠ A 8 7 6 4
          │      N      │      ♡ A K 2
          │  W       E  │      ◊ J 10 4
          │      S      │      ♣ Q 7
          └─────────────┘
```

I win with my ace and declarer, a jovial fellow with a bit of a beer belly, plays the five. What do think would make a good return?

One option is to switch to a diamond, playing partner for a singleton. My trump holding means that I must regain the lead before trumps are drawn. The snag is that Graham could have led a singleton diamond himself if he had one. What do you think of a club shift instead? With a third club, there might be some point but, even if I set up a club trick for partner, can you see any way to get him in to cash it?

A better idea seems to be to knock out the ♠K and play a forcing game. The clue comes from the time it took South to bid 4♡. Since he cannot have been thinking of bidding a different number of hearts, he must have had other options in mind. This implies that he is in a 4-3 fit.

Winning my spade return with the ♠K and throwing the ◊3 from dummy, declarer plays the ♡5 to the four and queen. Would you say it is a sensible idea to take this?

If I win and play a spade, dummy presumably ruffs. Even if declarer is also out of spades, he will want to take the ruff in the short hand. If dummy ruffs with the eight, I can duck the second round of trumps to leave the lead locked on the table. Then, assuming my theory that partner has three trumps holds true, a diamond ruff will provide the setting trick. The danger is that South has the ♡10-9-x-x. In that case, he can afford to ruff the spade high in dummy and overtake the ♡8 if I duck. It seems much better for me to duck the first round of trumps.

The ♡Q comes next, which I take with the king to return a spade. Declarer discards a club from hand and ruffs in dummy. Next comes the ♣A, to which all follow low, and three rounds of diamonds. Everyone follows to the first two rounds but partner ruffs the third. Declarer concedes one down at this point. He has lost three tricks and the ace of trumps is a sure loser. This was the full deal:

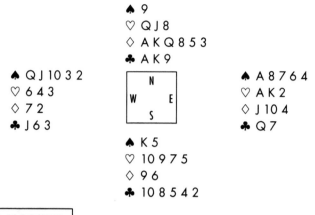

Once he was forced to ruff a spade in dummy, declarer's only hope lay in finding me with a doubleton ♣Q-J. On that layout there would be no way to stop him: if I ruffed the third round of clubs, it would be with a master; if instead I let him get to his hand, he could play a third round of trumps.

Later our teammates recounted an amusing tale. At their table, the bidding started the same way and the problem arose of what do after North's double of 3♠. South bid 3NT, intending it to show a hand suitable for play in two places (4♣ and 4♡), but North construed it as natural, not unreasonably you might say. 3NT proved unbeatable!

A number of developments in bidding theory have combined to make contracts played with a 4-3 trump fit less common than in the heyday of Sonny Moyse, who was famed for seeking such contracts. Five-card major openings, negative doubles after an overcall, false preference on the second round by responder and, where played, support doubles, are treatments that make it easier to avoid a 4-3 trump suit. The effect is that many people these days have limited experience of either playing in or defending against a 4-3 fit. At least as declarer you know when you are in a 4-3 fit. For the defenders, half the problem is identifying the fact.

In general, there are two specific ways to defend against a 4-3 fit. If declarer has short suits in both hands, you lead trumps to cut down the crossruff. If, as was the case here, declarer has a source of tricks on the side and wants to draw trumps, you play a forcing game. You stand a greater chance of success, of course, if one of you has four trumps.

Duplicate players quickly become familiar with the procedures for finding out the meaning of a conventional bid made by an opponent. If it is your turn to call (and you contemplate bidding), you can check their convention card or ask a question. If not, you can wait until your turn comes or you make the opening lead or, if partner ends up on lead, until the opening lead is face down on the table. Did you also know that it could pay to check the meaning of certain bids that nobody alerted?

Suppose you open 1NT and the next player bids 2♠. You may well want to know whether they play something like Astro (which covers all two-suited hands), when you can almost certainly place the overcaller with a six-card or longer suit, or whether they use Landy (2♣ for the majors), when a hand with 5-4 in spades and a minor is possible. Likewise, if you open 1◊ and the next player bids 1♠ now and 2♡ later, you will want to know not whether your opponents play Michaels cuebids (or Ghestem) and whether they use them on all hands with 5-5 in the majors.

In a Gold Cup match against competent opponents I pick up:

♠ 5　♡ K 9 7 5 3　◊ Q　♣ A Q J 10 9 2

Our side is vulnerable and I open 1♣. The player on my left overcalls 1♠ and my partner, Graham, makes a negative double. The next player bids 2♣, showing a value raise of spades, and I jump to 4♡. The overcaller, a lanky young man, bids 4♠. This ends the bidding:

WEST	NORTH	EAST	SOUTH
		1♣	1♠
dbl	2♣	4♡	4♠
all pass			

Partner leads the ♣5 and dummy appears as follows:

```
              ♠ A 4 3 2
              ♡ Q 10 4
              ◊ K 8 3
              ♣ K 8 3
         ┌──────────┐       ♠ 5
         │    N     │       ♡ K 9 7 5 3
         │ W     E  │       ◊ Q
         │    S     │       ♣ A Q J 10 9 2
         └──────────┘
```

Dummy plays low and the ♣9 wins, declarer following with the six. In our methods, the lead could come from ♣5-4, ♣6-5-4 or be a singleton. What would you return and what might you check on first?

A glance at the opponents' convention card uncovers two things: weak jump overcalls and Quantum, a way of showing any two-suited hand. This makes it likely that South has a single-suited hand too strong for a weak jump overcall. Partner's failure to double 4♠ is consistent with this.

If partner has a doubleton club, the ♡A and Q-10 of spades or similar, it will work to cash the ♣A, the ♡K and play a third club. South is unlikely to hold a singleton club because that would give him a two-suiter and, in any case, there seems little hope if we can make only one club trick.

I cash the ♣A and partner discards the ◇7. This is good news and bad news. The good is that he can ruff the next club. The bad is that we play odd cards as discouraging and, since he surely holds even cards in both red suits, he cannot hold a red ace. I intend to give him a ruff, so the size of my club should show suit-preference. With no fast entry in a red suit and not much minding which one he plays back, I lead the ♣J.

Graham ruffs and exits with the ♠K. Dummy wins with the ace and leads the ♡Q. What do you make of this? These are the cards on view:

```
        ♠ 4 3 2
        ♡ Q 10 4
        ◇ K 8 3
        ♣ —
    ┌─────────┐         ♠ —
    │    N    │         ♡ K 9 7 5 3
    │ W     E │         ◇ Q
    │    S    │         ♣ Q 10 2
    └─────────┘
```

Although a negative double does not guarantee four hearts, partner needs compensating values without them. Given that this appears impossible, declarer must have a singleton heart, the ace no doubt. I can see no point in covering, but can you see the danger of a squeeze on partner if we leave him to guard the hearts? He will need to protect the diamonds as well. After I duck, declarer sheepishly overtakes with the ace and runs the trumps, but we have no discarding problems. I keep hearts and partner diamonds to put the contract one down. This was the full deal:

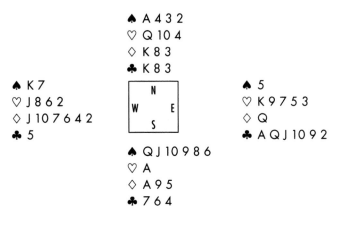

```
                    ♠ A 4 3 2
                    ♡ Q 10 4
                    ◇ K 8 3
                    ♣ K 8 3
  ♠ K 7                          ♠ 5
  ♡ J 8 6 2          N           ♡ K 9 7 5 3
  ◇ J 10 7 6 4 2  W     E        ◇ Q
  ♣ 5                S            ♣ A Q J 10 9 2
                    ♠ Q J 10 9 8 6
                    ♡ A
                    ◇ A 9 5
                    ♣ 7 6 4
```

POST MORTEM

Partner did well to exit with the ♠K after scoring his ruff. If he does anything else, declarer can unblock the ♡A before crossing to the ♠A and leading the ♡Q. I am then powerless to stop him from transferring the heart guard and partner will be squeezed on the run of the trumps:

```
                    ♠ —
                    ♡ 10
                    ◇ K 8
                    ♣ —
  ♠ —                            ♠ —
  ♡ J                N           ♡ 9 5
  ◇ J 10          W     E        ◇ —
  ♣ —                S            ♣ Q
                    ♠ 8
                    ♡ —
                    ◇ 9 5
                    ♣ —
```

You may have noticed that this book has a lower proportion of partscore deals than you might encounter at the table. In part, this results from the fact that they count for less and in part because you can less often place the unseen cards. You have to rely more on general principles, returning partner's suit and leading up to weakness, for instance. All the same, they can be important. At IMPs, two partscore swings can add up to as much as a game swing; at rubber bridge, two partscores can become a game; at matchpoints, partscore deals count for just as much as game and slam deals. Scoring well on a partscore deal often involves pushing the opponents a level higher than they would like and then defending well.

Playing in a charity (simultaneous) pairs, I am fourth in hand with both sides vulnerable when, as East, I pick up:

♠ K 9 7 5 3   ♡ 3   ◇ A K 3   ♣ J 8 7 6

South opens 1♡ and North responds 1NT. One option is to bid at once, but I would prefer better spades to bid 2♠ and am not keen on doubling with this shape and marginal values. When I pass, South rebids 2♡ and this comes back. Although doubling is possible, a likely result is that we play at the three-level in a 4-3 fit instead of in 2♠ on a 5-3 fit. I bid 2♠, and South takes the push the 3♡. We sell out now, having achieved the first goal of driving the opponents a level higher. The bidding has been:

WEST	NORTH	EAST	SOUTH
			1♡
pass	1NT	pass	2♡
pass	pass	2♠	3♡
all pass			

Partner leads the ♣K (not implying the ace) and dummy appears:

```
              ♠ J
              ♡ K 8
              ◇ 9 8 7 5 4
              ♣ Q 10 9 4 2
        ┌─────────────┐      ♠ K 9 7 5 3
        │      N      │      ♡ 3
        │  W       E  │      ◇ A K 3
        │      S      │      ♣ J 8 7 6
        └─────────────┘
```

My mother, Pam, who is my partner, would hardly lead an unsupported king on this auction and she surely has A-K doubleton. Since she cannot ruff just yet, I play the ♣8, normal count under the king. When she continues with the ace, I play my lowest club, the six, which this time is a suit-preference signal.

Seemingly getting the message (the singleton spade in dummy may have helped), she switches to the ◇J. I win with the king and the queen drops. This could be a true card, but I reflect that on a 4-6-1-2 shape South might have doubled 2♠ rather going to 3♡ (we are vulnerable and it is pairs). In addition, we may have got the bidding wrong if South is 3-7-1-2 and West is 4-3-4-2. Accordingly, I lead the ◇A next and, to my relief, it stands up. I switch back to clubs and, when declarer ruffs with the queen, partner discards a diamond. Next comes a heart to the ♡K and the ♠J. It would suit us for the lead to stay on the table, but declarer overtakes with the queen and ruffs a low spade in dummy. A diamond comes next and, when I follow, South ruffs high and my partner discards a spade. Then, after laying down a top trump on the next trick and seeing me show out, declarer concedes one down. This was the full deal:

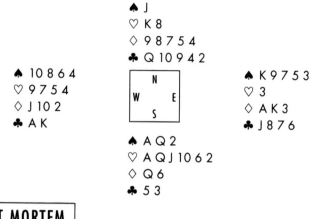

```
                    ♠ J
                    ♡ K 8
                    ◇ 9 8 7 5 4
                    ♣ Q 10 9 4 2
♠ 10 8 6 4          ┌─────────┐          ♠ K 9 7 5 3
♡ 9 7 5 4           │    N    │          ♡ 3
◇ J 10 2            │ W     E │          ◇ A K 3
♣ A K               │    S    │          ♣ J 8 7 6
                    └─────────┘
                    ♠ A Q 2
                    ♡ A Q J 10 6 2
                    ◇ Q 6
                    ♣ 5 3
```

POST MORTEM

As the cards lie, 3♠ is makeable, even if the defenders play three rounds of trumps, but only by dropping the ◇Q. With four hearts and four spades, partner probably did well to defend. With both sides vulnerable, you do not want to buy the contract and go down on a partscore deal if there is any risk of being doubled, which clearly there was here.

Although the opening lead was obvious, partner did well later. She switched to a diamond rather than the suit I had bid and worked out to throw her winning ◇10 on the third club to set up an overruff. For my part, cashing the ◇K rather than letting declarer throw a diamond on the third round of clubs was fairly routine. However, you do not always need to cash your side winners before trying for a trump promotion. Consider this deal:

```
                    ♠ 7
                    ♡ A K Q
                    ◇ K Q 6
                    ♣ 10 9 7 6 5 2
♠ K 9 5             ┌─────────┐          ♠ 6
♡ 10 8 5 4 3        │    N    │          ♡ J 7 6 2
◇ 10 8 5 4          │ W     E │          ◇ A 7 3
♣ 3                 │    S    │          ♣ A K J 8 4
                    └─────────┘
                    ♠ A Q J 10 8 4 3 2
                    ♡ 9
                    ◇ J 9 2
                    ♣ Q
```

South opens and plays in 4♠, and West leads the ♣3 to East's king. Cashing the ◇A before returning a club will defeat the contract if West's trumps are at least as good as A-10-x, K-10-x, A-9-x-x, K-9-x-x or Q-9-x-x. On the actual layout, taking the ◇A does not work. Declarer ruffs the second round of clubs with the ♠Q and loses only one trump trick. East needs to play a club straight back. South ruffs high and West correctly discards. Then, after a heart to the ace and a spade to the queen and king, a diamond lead puts East back on lead and a third round of clubs promotes the ♠9. This sequence defeats the contract if West's trumps are A-9-x, K-9-x, A-8-x-x, K-8-x-x or Q-8-x-x or better. There is little risk attached to retaining the ◇A, because it would only run away if South has nine spades. In that case the contract figures to be unbeatable.

Twenty or twenty-five years ago, strong club systems enjoyed widespread support and for many young players the question was not whether to play a strong club system but which one to play. The Italians won many World Championships using Blue Club and, as you may know or have read in *The Bridge Bum* by Alan Sontag, the Aces Team used Precision to great effect. Both systems have fallen into decline, partly because you cannot use them in cut-in bridge and partly because nobody teaches them. Also, once the proportion of players familiar with them went below a critical level, you could no longer use them in casual partnerships. I bet, though, that they will enjoy a resurgence if ever five-card majors and the strong notrump become the norm right across the world. There will always be people who want to do something different from the majority. I am glad that, for now, Meckstroth-Rodwell are carrying the torch.

Playing in the regular duplicate at the Cambridge University Bridge Club, neither side is vulnerable when I pick up this modest collection:

♠ 10 8 4   ♡ J 8 4   ◇ A 10 8 4   ♣ 10 7 4

My partner, Neil, as West, opens 2◇. In Precision, this shows a three-suiter short in diamonds. For us, 4-4-1-4, 4-4-0-5 or, with poor clubs, 3-4-1-5 or 4-3-1-5 are all fine. North doubles and I am happy to pass. After South also passes, Neil redoubles for rescue and I run to 2♡. South competes to 3◇ and North considers bidding on but passes. The bidding has been:

WEST	NORTH	EAST	SOUTH
2◇	dbl	pass	pass
redbl	pass	2♡	3◇
all pass			

Partner leads the ♡K and dummy comes down.

♠ A Q J 9
♡ A 5 2
◇ J 5 3
♣ A 5 3

```
        N
    W       E
        S
```

♠ 10 8 4
♡ J 8 4
◇ A 10 8 4
♣ 10 7 4

The ace wins and I encourage with the eight. Dummy leads a trump and this goes to the four, king and nine. A spade, the six, comes next, and this goes seven, queen and four. Dummy leads another trump and it seems natural for me to play low — going in with the ace would blow my second trump trick. Declarer, a bearded natural science student, wins with the queen, while partner discards the ♡7. Then declarer takes a second spade finesse and throws a heart on the ♠A. Next he ruffs the ♠9, as I discard a low club, and then leads the ♡10. These are the cards left on view:

♠ —
♡ 5 2
◇ J
♣ A 5 3

```
        N
    W       E
        S
```

♠ —
♡ J 4
◇ A 10
♣ 10 7

Partner pauses and I count seven tricks for declarer already: the ♡A, three spades, the ◇K-Q and a spade ruff. Since the ♣A must score, a heart ruff in his hand will be his ninth trick. Obviously, declarer is hoping either that the lead was from ♡K-Q-J or that we will misdefend. Fortunately, Neil does the right thing, playing low. Maybe he recalls the ♡8 I played under the ace or that I might have thrown a heart without the ♡J.

Winning the heart with the jack, it is clear what to do. I cash the ◇A, on which partner discards the ♣9, and then play the ◇10, on which he throws the ♡9. Now, knowing that Neil has one heart and two clubs left, it must be right to lead a club in case his clubs are K-J rather than K-Q. As it happens, my play at this point makes no difference: Neil has the ♣K-Q and the contract goes down. This was the full deal:

```
                    ♠ A Q J 9
                    ♡ A 5 2
                    ◇ J 5 3
                    ♣ A 5 3
  ♠ K 7 3 2         ┌─────────┐        ♠ 10 8 4
  ♡ K Q 9 7         │    N    │        ♡ J 8 4
  ◇ 9               │ W     E │        ◇ A 10 8 4
  ♣ K Q 9 6         │    S    │        ♣ 10 7 4
                    └─────────┘
                    ♠ 6 5
                    ♡ 10 6 3
                    ◇ K Q 7 6 2
                    ♣ J 8 2
```

POST MORTEM

In the bar afterwards, we spot that as the play went declarer could have made the contract. However, we should not have given him the chance.

```
                    ♠ 9
                    ♡ 5 2
                    ◇ J
                    ♣ A 5 3
  ♠ K               ┌─────────┐        ♠ —
  ♡ Q 9             │    N    │        ♡ J 4
  ◇ —               │ W     E │        ◇ A 10
  ♣ K Q 9 6         │    S    │        ♣ 10 7 4
                    └─────────┘
                    ♠ —
                    ♡ 10
                    ◇ 7 6 2
                    ♣ J 8 2
```

Instead of ruffing the fourth spade, declarer might have discarded his ♡10, making sure that I could not gain the lead. After West wins and leads the ♣K, declarer ducks to leave West endplayed, forced to lead a heart. The ♣A provides an entry for ruffing another round of hearts.

Can you see how to stop this from happening? Hopping up with the ◇A on the second round does it! I can then switch to a club, or we can cash one or two hearts, ending in my hand, before switching to a club. In each case, declarer loses two hearts, two clubs and the ◇A; alternatively, if he elects to overtake the ◇J, he loses two trumps and three tricks in hearts and clubs.

'Hi Eddie Kantar,

I came across a deal the other day that you should find of interest because one of the pairs at least must have been reading your great book on slam bidding, *Roman Keycard Blackwood*:

Second in hand and vulnerable against not, you hold:

♠ A 7 2   ♡ Q 9 4   ◇ —   ♣ A J 8 7 6 5 2

The hand on your right opens one heart and you overcall two clubs. I'm not sure you'd bid more even at other vulnerabilities. The hand on your left bids two diamonds and when partner passes, RHO makes a splinter bid of four clubs. I assume you pass over that, and now comes the bid you have been waiting for. South bids 4NT. Is it right to say that 4◇ would be Roman Keycard Blackwood and so this is to play?'

'Yes, 4◇ should be RKB (assuming they play the splinter as a game force) and, yes, 4NT should be to play. The main gain of using 4◇ as the ask is that none of the normal replies will take the bidding above five of the agreed suit. The fact that it leaves 4NT free to be natural is a bonus.'

'Great. RHO bids 5♣, no doubt showing a void in clubs rather than a singleton, and LHO jumps to 6◇. This completes the bidding:

WEST	NORTH	EAST	SOUTH
	1♡	2♣	2◇
pass	4♣	pass	4NT
pass	5♣	pass	6◇
all pass			

Partner leads the ten of clubs and dummy is as follows:

```
            ♠ K Q J 9
            ♡ A K 8 6 3
            ◇ Q J 10 6
            ♣ —
        ┌─────────┐        ♠ A 7 2
        │    N    │        ♡ Q 9 4
        │ W     E │        ◇ —
        │    S    │        ♣ A J 8 7 6 5 2
        └─────────┘
```

Dummy ruffs the club low and leads the queen of trumps. You discard a club and the other players follow low. After a pause, declarer continues with the king of spades from dummy. If you win, what do you return? If you duck, partner shows you an odd number of spades and the ♠Q comes next. Again, do you win, and, if you do, what do you return?'

'I duck the first spade and win the second. It sounds impossible on the bidding that South, who tried to sign off in 4NT, can have a singleton spade. I then return a spade to kill an entry to dummy. I am playing South for the K-Q of clubs and the ace-king of diamonds in a 3-2-5-3 shape. Declarer can no longer set up the hearts and, if he doesn't have the ◊9, he can't get home on a crossruff either.'

'Yes, holding up the first spade does the trick and you are right about declarer's shape. With a 3-1-5-4 shape, it would still be possible to make the slam by a dummy reversal, ruffing two hearts low in hand and drawing trumps ending in dummy. This was the full deal:'

```
                    ♠ K Q J 9
                    ♡ A K 8 6 3
                    ◊ Q J 10 6
                    ♣ —
   ♠ 10 4 3                              ♠ A 7 2
   ♡ 10 7 5          N                   ♡ Q 9 4
   ◊ 9 7 5 4      W     E                ◊ —
   ♣ 10 9 3          S                   ♣ A J 8 7 6 5 2
                    ♠ 8 6 5
                    ♡ J 2
                    ◊ A K 8 3 2
                    ♣ K Q 4
```

Usually when both sides play the same suit, in this case spades, someone is making a mistake. Here, exceptionally, the play made sense for both sides. After the bad trump split came to light, declarer worked out that it would be necessary to knock out the ♠A before drawing trumps. Indeed, there was a chance of a squeeze if East was 2-4-0-7. Next East, after winning the spade, had to return the suit to kill the entry to the long hearts. In fact, since South held the ♡J, East had no safe exit anyway other than in spades.

Perhaps you are wondering whether it would prove equally effective for East to duck both the first and the second round of spades. Well, if that happens, declarer can cash the ace and king of hearts and ruff the third round with a baby trump to reach this position:

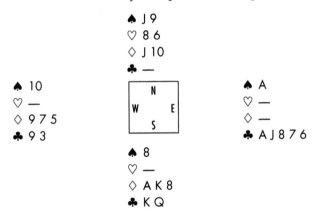

```
                        ♠ J 9
                        ♡ 8 6
                        ◇ J 10
                        ♣ —
        ♠ 10                            ♠ A
        ♡ —         ┌──────────┐        ♡ —
        ◇ 9 7 5     │ W    N   │        ◇ —
        ♣ 9 3       │      E   │        ♣ A J 8 7 6
                    │    S     │
                    └──────────┘
                        ♠ 8
                        ♡ —
                        ◇ A K 8
                        ♣ K Q
```

The hearts are set up, but it is no good attempting to enjoy them. Instead, declarer ruffs a club in dummy and ruffs a heart high in hand. West will probably discard a club at this point and a spade when declarer ruffs a club with dummy's last trump. However, now West has only trumps left. He has to ruff the next trick and return a trump into South's tenace.

Nor, of course, does it help West to ruff or underruff to avoid the trump endplay. In this case, having taken the final club ruff, declarer discards the ♠8 on a long heart. After West ruffs, the ◇9 will be singleton and again the defenders make a trump trick but nothing else. So one can conclude that ducking two spades would work if West held ◇9-8-x-x but not on the actual layout.

Varied Approach 58

If you have ever attended a fire safety course, you may know the (slightly tricky) answer to the question: 'When is a door not a door?' The answer is simple, of course: 'When it is a jar'. In bridge, you might ask: 'When is an exit card not an exit card?' The answer to that can be complicated. Let's try the easier question: 'When is an entry not an entry?' The answer is: 'When it is in a suit declarer need not play and partner cannot play.'

In the main teams event at a congress on the South Coast I pick up:

♠ K 6   ♡ K 8 3   ◇ 7 6 4   ♣ A Q J 10 4

Both sides are vulnerable and, since we are playing a strong notrump when vulnerable, I open 1♣. The lady on my left overcalls 1◇ and she finds herself in 3NT after this bidding:

WEST	NORTH	EAST	SOUTH
		1♣	1◇
pass	1♡	pass	1NT
pass	2NT	pass	3NT
all pass			

My partner, David, leads the ♣5 and this is what we see on the table:

```
            ♠ J 10 9 7
            ♡ A 10 9 6 4
            ◇ A Q 8
            ♣ 8
      ┌─────────────┐        ♠ K 6
      │      N      │        ♡ K 8 3
      │  W       E  │        ◇ 7 6 4
      │      S      │        ♣ A Q J 10 4
      └─────────────┘
```

Unable to see any advantage in taking the ace, I play the ten. This wins when South plays the three. In our methods, and assuming South holds the ♣K for her 1NT bid, the ♣5 lead could be from 6-5-2, 7-5-2, 9-5-2 or 5-2. 9-5-3-2 and 7-5-3-2 are no longer possible now that she has played the three. This makes it highly likely that she began with ♣K-x-x-x.

I return the ♣Q, trying to maintain communications with partner, and the play to this trick confirms my suspicion about the club suit. South plays the six and West the seven, as dummy discards a heart. It is certain now that she has king and a low club left. What do you think of playing ace and another club at this point? Do you agree that some counting should precede an action like that? These cards remain:

```
              ♠ J 10 9 7
              ♡ A 10 9 6
              ◇ A Q 8
              ♣ —
        ┌─────────┐    ♠ K 6
        │    N    │    ♡ K 8 3
        │ W     E │    ◇ 7 6 4
        │    S    │    ♣ A J 4
        └─────────┘
```

Since an overcall on ◇K-J-x-x would be most odd, declarer must have at least five diamond tricks. If I play another club, she will score a club trick and then there is the ♡A in dummy. This gives her seven tricks and, if she is to develop two more without letting me in, she will need two spade tricks. Obviously, we stand no chance if she has the ace and queen of spades. The trouble is that she only needs ♠A-x to make two tricks if not three, and it will seem more attractive to finesse a spade into David's hand rather than a heart into mine. In practical terms, clearing the clubs relies on finding partner with the ♠A. This sounds most unlikely on the bidding, leaving South with at best an aceless 12-count for her 1NT rebid and advance to game, and with her accompanying ♠Q-x of spades and ♡Q-J hardly pulling full weight. My best chance, surely, lies in finding her with ♠A-x-x and a singleton heart. In case her heart is the queen, I switch to the ♡K.

South does play the queen under my king, partner playing the five, and the ace wins. Declarer then leads the ♡10 off dummy and discards a spade. Partner wins with the jack and returns the two to dummy's nine. Declarer discards a club on the third heart and runs five rounds of diamonds. This gives me no problem. I keep ♠K-x and the ♣A. She finishes with the ♠A in the forlorn hope of dropping the ♠K and ♠Q together. My ♠K and ♣A win the last two tricks to put the contract one down. This was the full deal:

```
              ♠ J 10 9 7
              ♡ A 10 9 6 4
              ◇ A Q 8
              ♣ 8
♠ Q 5 4 2      ┌─────────┐      ♠ K 6
♡ J 7 5 2      │    N    │      ♡ K 8 3
◇ 5 2          │ W     E │      ◇ 7 6 4
♣ 7 5 2        │    S    │      ♣ A Q J 10 4
              └─────────┘
              ♠ A 8 3
              ♡ Q
              ◇ K J 10 9 3
              ♣ K 9 6 3
```

POST MORTEM

The key to defeating the contract came from working out the need
to switch because partner had the relevant entry. Another situation
in which you might switch to a new suit, if only temporarily, is
when you can see that continuing the first will not develop enough
tricks. Consider this example:

```
              ♠ J 5
              ♡ K Q 10 6
              ◇ Q 6
              ♣ A J 10 6 4
♠ A 10 7 2     ┌─────────┐      ♠ K 8 6 3
♡ 9 8 4 2      │    N    │      ♡ 7 5
◇ K 9 3        │ W     E │      ◇ J 8 5 4 2
♣ 8 2          │    S    │      ♣ K 5
              └─────────┘
              ♠ Q 9 4
              ♡ A J 3
              ◇ A 10 7
              ♣ Q 9 7 3
```

South, having opened a weak 1NT or responded 3NT to 1♣, plays
in 3NT. West leads the ♠2 (fourth best) and the king wins. As East,
you can see four tricks by clearing the spades — three spades and a
club — not enough. You need a diamond as well and should return
the ◇8. South has to duck and the king wins. West now reverts to
spades, a clue for this being your choice of the high ◇8 to deny
interest in diamonds.

When playing rubber bridge, Chicago (four-deal bridge) or IMPs and defending an undoubled contract, your main target is normally clear: to defeat the contract. The position becomes more complicated at matchpoints or board-a-match (point-a-board) scoring. Saving an overtrick may suffice to give you a good score, whilst taking a contract one off may not be enough if other people beat it by more. In such cases, you need to assess your target in light of dummy's strength and, for deciding whether you need multiple undertricks, the value of contracts available your way.

A similar position arises at any scoring with a doubled contract. Should you look for a big set or should you content yourself with one down? Again, you need to assess your target in the context of the information available to you. In 'Clear the Way', it became clear at an early stage in the play that a big penalty was in the offing and you could concentrate on looking for the maximum. By contrast, in 'Close Double' you could see from dummy that achieving just one down would require some luck.

With neither side vulnerable in a charity pairs, I am pleased to pick up:

♠ A Q 9 5 ♡ 7 ◇ A 10 5 4 2 ♣ A K 5

The dealer on my left, South, a recently retired gentleman, opens 4♡. Two passes follow and I reopen with a double. With support for the other three suits and four and a half possible defensive tricks, I do not mind whether partner removes the double or not. In the event, the bidding ends there:

WEST	NORTH	EAST	SOUTH
			4♡
pass	pass	dbl	all pass

My partner, John, leads the ♣J and this is what we see:

```
            ♠ J 10 4 3
            ♡ A Q 6
            ◇ K 9
            ♣ 9 7 3 2
      ┌───────────┐
      │     N     │        ♠ A Q 9 5
      │ W       E │        ♡ 7
      │     S     │        ◇ A 10 5 4 2
      └───────────┘        ♣ A K 5
```

Naturally, I win with the ♣K and the queen drops. This may or may not be a true card. What do you think is the correct return here?

Dummy's strength suggests we should just look to beat the contract. I count three sure tricks — John would have bid 4♠ with ♠K-x-x-x-x and it seems unlikely he has six diamonds. We may have a second club trick, although it can hardly run away. Our other main chance is that John has the ◇Q. Since there is a danger of running short of exit cards, I do not wish to help declarer strip them by returning a club. I return a trump, to which all follow. Dummy wins with the queen and leads a low spade, putting me back on the spot. Here are some possible hands for declarer:

```
♠ K                      ♠ K                      ♠ K 7
♡ K J 10 9 5 4 3 2       ♡ K J 10 9 5 4 3 2       ♡ K J 10 9 5 4 3 2
◇ Q 7                    ◇ J 7                    ◇ J 7
♣ Q 4                    ♣ Q 4                    ♣ Q
```

Against the first hand, I need to play the ace of spades and cash the ace of clubs. Against the second hand, we may do even better if I win the spade, underlead my ♣A, and have declarer put to a guess when partner shifts to a diamond. We still beat the contract if I duck the spade because this leaves declarer two diamond losers. For the third hand, I must duck the spade to avoid setting up a ruffing finesse against my ♠Q.

The second hand seems unlikely. Why would declarer kindly give us communication in clubs? In any case, ducking still beats the contract by one. Which of the other two do you think is more likely? Even if declarer would always falsecard with ♣Q-x, three ♣Q-x holdings are possible but four of ♠K-x. This alone makes it better to play for the third hand. Once one adds in the fact that South may not drop the queen from ♣Q-x and that ducking works better if South has three spades, it seems clear to do so. The ♠K wins and I am pleased to see John play the ♠2, showing an odd number.

Declarer pauses before leading up to the ♠J. I win and lead the ♣A, which he ruffs. Then, when he leads the ♡K and overtakes with the ♡A, partner discards a club and I throw away a diamond. Next comes the ♠4, on which I play the ♠9. After ruffing this, declarer tries the ◇J. John covers with the queen and we win two diamonds for one down. This was the full deal:

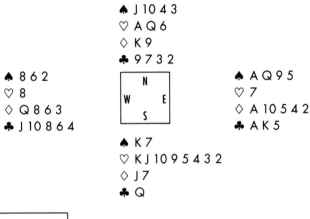

```
              ♠ J 10 4 3
              ♡ A Q 6
              ◇ K 9
              ♣ 9 7 3 2
♠ 8 6 2                        ♠ A Q 9 5
♡ 8              N             ♡ 7
◇ Q 8 6 3    W       E         ◇ A 10 5 4 2
♣ J 10 8 6 4       S           ♣ A K 5
              ♠ K 7
              ♡ K J 10 9 5 4 3 2
              ◇ J 7
              ♣ Q
```

POST MORTEM

It would have done declarer no good to use dummy's second heart entry to ruff a club instead. I still have a club left with which to exit after scoring my spade trick. If, however, I lead the ♣A and have it ruffed at Trick 2, the contract might well make. After a trump to dummy, a spade to the king, a trump back to dummy and a third round of clubs ruffed high, the next spade would endplay me in the position below. Winning with the ♠A and returning the ♠9 is best, but South can discard a diamond.

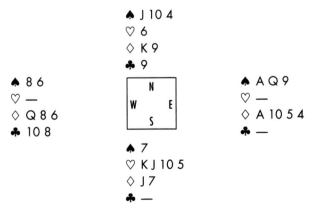

```
              ♠ J 10 4
              ♡ 6
              ◇ K 9
              ♣ 9
♠ 8 6                          ♠ A Q 9
♡ —              N             ♡ —
◇ Q 8 6      W       E         ◇ A 10 5 4
♣ 10 8             S           ♣ —
              ♠ 7
              ♡ K J 10 5
              ◇ J 7
              ♣ —
```

Patience Rewarded 60

One of my claims to fame (shared with Cameron Small, I believe) is that, despite having won three junior trials, I never played for the Great Britain Under 25 team. At the time it felt a great injustice but, in a world in which some have too little to eat or no access to safe drinking water, it now seems a small cross to bear. Besides, by not playing much international bridge, I've had time for a wonderful wife, Helen, four lovely children and to see some of the world's most beautiful places – Crater Lake, Spirit Island, Milford Sound and Ayers Rock, for example. Finally, I've had the chance to work with some of the game's greatest players and writers.

♠ Q J 4 3   ♡ J 10 4 2   ◊ 8   ♣ Q 7 6 4

In a match against fellow students, I pick up this hand. The other side is vulnerable and the bidding, with 2NT showing 18-19, unfolds as follows:

WEST	NORTH	EAST	SOUTH
pass	pass	pass	1◊
pass	1♠	pass	2NT
pass	3NT	all pass	

My partner, Doug, leads the ♣2 (fourth best) and this is what we see:

```
            ♠ 9 8 6 5
            ♡ A 9
            ◊ Q J 9 5
            ♣ J 10 3
       N              ♠ Q J 4 3
    W     E           ♡ J 10 4 2
       S              ◊ 8
                      ♣ Q 7 6 4
```

Dummy plays the jack and I must decide whether to cover. It will be right to do so if the lead comes from A-K-x-x. How likely do you think that is? For one thing, Doug might have led a high card from such a holding. For another, South might have chosen a different rebid, 2♡ perhaps, with two low clubs. Finally, we seem to have little hope if partner has 7 points in clubs. The bidding limits him to 8 in all (I can see 14 and South has shown at least 18). If South

198 DEFEND THESE HANDS WITH ME

has the remaining cards, I can count nine tricks: two spades, three hearts and four diamonds. Since ducking can gain if the lead comes from ♣A-x-x-x and should cost little otherwise, it must be right to encourage with the seven.

After the ♣J wins and South plays the nine, dummy leads the ◊Q. This holds as well, partner playing the seven. The ◊J comes next and I must find a discard. People say that 4441 types are tough to bid. They are difficult to defend with as well! Since partner's ◊7 must show an even number, presumably four, we need three discards. Assuming that he began with the hoped-for four clubs to the ace, I can count the shape of the unseen hands. He must be 2-3-4-4 and South 3-4-4-2. Doug will also need to hold the ♠A or the ♡K, but it as not yet clear which of these he holds. If South has ♠A-K-x, a spade discard will be unsafe because then three rounds will set up a long spade. Likewise, if South holds ♡K-Q-x-x, a heart discard will cost. Despite the risk of blocking the suit, I decide to defer the decision by throwing a club.

Doug helpfully drops the ◊10 on the second diamond, showing that he has the ♠A. I discard a low spade on the third round of diamonds. What do you suggest throwing on the fourth? These are the cards left:

```
            ♠ 9 8 6 5
            ♡ A 9
            ◊ 9
            ♣ 10 3
        ┌─────────┐      ♠ Q J 3
        │    N    │      ♡ J 10 4 2
        │ W     E │      ◊ —
        │    S    │      ♣ Q 6
        └─────────┘
```

Clearly, a club is wrong — dummy's ten would become good. In view of the fall of the ♣9 at Trick 1, if South has two clubs left, then they will be the K-8. If so, we cannot beat the contract. So, putting South with four hearts, I cannot spare a heart. It seems natural to throw the ♠3 but the blockage worries me. Suppose declarer crosses to the ♡A and leads a spade to the king and ace. Doug can cash the ♣A, felling the king, and play a club to my queen. Sadly, declarer then has time to set up a long spade.

Although it could look silly if South has ♠K-10-x, since there is only one chance in three that partner holds ♠A-10 doubleton, I release the ♠Q. As expected, declarer crosses to the ♡A and leads a spade. I hop up with the ♠J to make sure I do not win the second round, and this goes to the king and ace. Partner cashes the ♣A and the ♣K drops. He plays a third club to my queen. The moment of truth has arrived and I lead my last spade. My luck is in. Partner produces the ten and cashes the last club to put the contract one down. This was the full deal:

```
                    ♠ 9 8 6 5
                    ♡ A 9
                    ◇ Q J 9 5
                    ♣ J 10 3
    ♠ A 10                              ♠ Q J 4 3
    ♡ 8 6 5          ┌─────────┐        ♡ J 10 4 2
    ◇ 10 7 4 2       │    N    │        ◇ 8
    ♣ A 8 5 2        │ W     E │        ♣ Q 7 6 4
                     │    S    │
                     └─────────┘
                    ♠ K 7 2
                    ♡ K Q 7 3
                    ◇ A K 6 3
                    ♣ K 9
```

POST MORTEM

In theory, West might have dropped the ◇10 on the first round to signal for spades, but suit-preference then would not be standard. As the play went, this was the position we reached when I had to discard the ♠Q:

```
                    ♠ 9 8 6 5
                    ♡ A 9
                    ◇ 9
                    ♣ 10 3
    ♠ A 10                              ♠ Q J 3
    ♡ 8 6 5          ┌─────────┐        ♡ J 10 4 2
    ◇ 4              │    N    │        ◇ —
    ♣ A 8 5          │ W     E │        ♣ Q 6
                     │    S    │
                     └─────────┘
                    ♠ K 7 2
                    ♡ K Q 7 3
                    ◇ K
                    ♣ K
```

Playing a high spade could easily have cost an overtrick (1 IMP), but the risk was surely worth it for the chance of a set (12 IMPs).

CPSIA information can be obtained
at www.ICGtesting.com
Printed in the USA
LVOW10s0600130218
566386LV00026B/291/P